JAMES THE JUST
IN
THE HABAKKUK *PESHER*

STUDIA POST-BIBLICA

INSTITUTA A P. A. H. DE BOER

ADIUVANTIBUS

L.R.A. VAN ROMPAY ET J. SMIT SIBINGA

EDIDIT

J. C. H. LEBRAM

VOLUMEN TRICESIMUM QUINTUM

LEIDEN

E. J. BRILL

1986

JAMES THE JUST
IN
THE HABAKKUK *PESHER*

BY

ROBERT H. EISENMAN

LEIDEN
E. J. BRILL
1986

ISBN   90 04 07587 9

CONTENTS

INTRODUCTION

This work is the second in a series attempting to develop a more secure foundation for studying Qumran origins and moving Second Temple historiography into a new framework, *i.e.*, seeing the sectarian situation as Qumran would have seen it and not from the point-of-view of the more familiar traditions that have come down to us. *Maccabees, Zadokites, Christians and Qumran: A New Hypothesis of Qumran Origins*, Leiden, 1983 treated the relationship of James the Just to the Qumran Community at some length and proposed new conceptual and historical parameters for viewing some of the problems associated with Qumran research. It set forth the connections of the Righteousness doctrine with the Zadokite Priesthood, in the process making the case for an esoteric or qualitative —even an eschatological—exegesis of the ''Zadokite Covenant'' and the twin concepts of *Hesed* (''Piety towards God'') and *Zedek* (''Righteousness towards men'') as the fundamental orientation of all ''opposition'' groups in this period.

In attempting to tie the terminology ''Pharisees'' closer to the group intended by the Qumran circumlocution, ''Seekers after Smooth Things,'' a more generic definition of the Pharisees was proposed and both groups were viewed as coextensive with those ''seeking accommodation with foreigners'' (inclusive of Herodians and Romans—at Qumran ''ʿamim'' and ''yeter ha-ʿamim''). In doing so, some terminological and historical confusions between ''Pharisees'' and ''Essenes'' were pointed up, and Qumran palaeography and archaeology were subjected to thoroughgoing criticism. Once the import of these re-evaluations was appreciated, I suggested that it was a comparatively easy task to link the events and teachings of the Righteous Teacher in the Habakkuk *Pesher* to those of James the Just in the early ''Jerusalem Community''.

James the Just in the Habakkuk Pesher is the application of the theory to the special case (an appendix extends it to both the Zadokite Document and Temple Scroll). Providing the kind of detailed exposition, specific identifications, and substantive argumentation necessary to support the overall thesis, it analyses the Habakkuk *Pesher* passage by passage, systematically signalling the connections between the life and teachings of James the Just and those of the Righteous Teacher of Qumran.

Not only was the ''Righteousness'' ideal integrally associated with James' being (*i.e.*, he was a Teacher of Righteousness and the sobriquet ''the Just '' or ''Righteous One'' was attached in an integral manner to his name), but early Church sources also confirm that scriptural exegesis of a Qumran kind was carried on with regard to his person ("and the Prophets declare concerning him"; *E.H.* 2.23.8—the actual passage applied to James' death being Is 3:10, a *zaddik* passage paralleling the sense and signification of *zaddik* passages like Hab 1-2 and Ps 37 applied at Qumran to the death of the Righteous Teacher). The Pseudoclementines actually place James together with *all* his community in the Jericho area in the early forties, from where he sends out Peter to confront Simon *Magus* in Caesarea (not "Samaria" as per the here weaker Acts tradition). Paralleling John the Baptist's earlier confrontation with Herodians, the confrontation bears on the themes of marriage, divorce, and "fornication" and links up with data in Josephus suggesting Simon to have been in the employ of Herodians/Romans and connived at Drusilla's legally reprehensible divorce and remarriage to Felix.

Two antagonists are also readily discernible with regard to James' life. One was an establishment high priest responsible for his death—Ananus. Ananus was killed in the early stages of the uprising by "Violent Gentiles" and his body was violated and thrown outside the walls of Jerusalem without burial (events we think are reflected in the Habakkuk *Pesher*); the other, a self-willed, often rebellious and argumentative individual within the movement, Paul. Following a more antinomian approach to the Law, he had a new version of "salvation" which he proposed "teaching to the Gentiles". These two antagonists of James can be linked to the *two antagonists* of the Righteous Teacher in the Habakkuk *Pesher*: one a "Man of Lying"/"Pourer out of Lying" within the community itself, who "speaks derogatorily about the Law in the midst of the whole congregation," "leads Many astray"/"tires out Many with a worthless service" (the opposite of the Righteous Teacher's proper "justifying" activity of "making Many Righteous"), and "leads astray in a wilderness without a Way" (the opposite of 1QS,viii.27's proper *teaching* activity of "making a Way in the wilderness" by showing "zeal for the Law"/*hok*). In the context of terminological allusions such as these and their doctrinal reversal or inversion in the New Testament, one should not forget Acts 21:21's description of the majority of James' "Jerusalem Church" supporters as "zealous for the Law").

The *pesher*, in addition to accusing the establishment high priest it refers to as "Wicked" of being responsible for the death of the Righteous Teacher, also charges him with "polluting the Temple". This charge comprised one of the "three nets of Belial" following the exegesis of the "Zadokite Covenant" in CD,iv-v (the other two: "fornication" and "Riches" have *real* applications to Herodians, as opposed to artificial ones to Maccabeans and others; both are echoed in the *pesher*). Two persistent themes relating to the personal status of Herodians also exercised

Qumran legal theorists in the Zadokite Document and Temple Scroll, *divorce* and *marrying nieces*. Together with a third theme, incest, they bear on the "fornication" charge above. Antagonism to "fornication" is a significant theme, too, in all extant traditions attaching themselves to James' name. In the Appendix, we shall be able to delineate the provenance of these "fornication" and "pollution of the Temple" charges with some precision, together with their culmination and combination in the Zadokite Document's curious charge of "sleeping with women in their periods".

In the Habakkuk *Pesher*, it will become clear that the "polluting the Temple" charge relates to accepting gifts (and sacrifices) from Herodians and other *violent* Gentiles, as well as incurring their "pollution" by associating with them. Priests like Ananus, it should be remembered, took their appointment from Herodians, who from the time of Herod the Great shared possession of the high priest's vestments with the Procurators, and their guilt therefore was one of association. Another aspect of the "pollution" charge was the fact that Herodians were even allowed into the Temple, a theme which is at the center of the internecine squabbling from the 40's to the 60's C.E., triggering the uprising against Rome. The problem of Herodians in the Temple will ultimately have to be seen, Qumran palaeography notwithstanding, as being at the root of the allusion to improper "separation" introducing the Zadokite Document's "sleeping with women in their periods" and the Temple Scroll's "*balla^c*"/"Bela^c"/"things sacrificed to idols" interdiction materials.

Perhaps even more importantly, I suggest that what can only be understood as the "Jerusalem Church" or "Palestinian" version of the exegesis of Hab 2:4 is present in the *pesher*. In our view, the presence in the *pesher* of this much-overlooked exegesis is the real reason for its composition. Framed as if with the "empty" or "guilty" exposition of "the Liar" in mind, the Habakkuk *Pesher* restricts the efficacy of this exegesis in a two-fold manner, firstly only to "the House of Judah" (*i.e.*, *only to native Jews*) and secondly, only to "*Torah*-Doers" (in this context, one should pay attention to the parallel reiteration of the "Doers" theme in the first chapter of the Letter of James, a letter also alluding to Qumran "empty", "Lying", and "Jewish Christian" "Enemy" terminologies, and an additional one, echoed at Qumran, "the Tongue"). Like the eschatological sense of the Zadokite exegesis, the eschatological sense of the Hab 2:4 *pesher*'s "saved from the *Beit ha-Mishpat*" has escaped many commentators. In addition, the *pesher* retains James' all-important soteriological stress on "works" along with the more familiar one on "belief".

We shall also be able to develop the meaning of other important turns-of-phrase at Qumran, like "*nilveh*"/"*nilvim*" in the Nahum *Pesher* and the Zadokite Document, which confirm the existence of a cadre of "God-fearers" attached to the Qumran Community. This, in turn, will clarify the decipherment of allusions in the Nahum *Pesher* like the "Simple Ones of Ephraim" (as opposed to those "of Judah", bearing on terminologies like "these Little Ones" and "the First" vs. "the Last" in the Gospels—extant at Qumran with varying signification), the "City of Blood" in the Nahum and Habakkuk *Peshers*, and the "*'Arizei-Go'im*" in the Ps 37 *Pesher*, not to mention the all-important allusions to "Belial" in the Zadokite Document and Hymns (and their probable esoteric variation in the "*balla'*"/"Bela'" usage in the Temple Scroll), almost all in one way or another involving Gentiles. The Temple Scroll refers, as well, to "things sacrificed to idols", a central category of James' directives to overseas communities (later echoed even in Koranic recitations of similar prohibitive categories).

In applying the general theory outlined in *Maccabees* to the special case of the Habakkuk *Pesher*, we are able to interpret or translate in a meaningful manner almost every passage and turn-of-phrase in the context of known facts about James' life and doctrines associated with him. This ability to explain key allusions at Qumran constitutes the kind of persuasive evidence the verification of the whole requires. It is as if one were predicting a certain effect, and having predicted it, indeed, finding it in the text. This is the import, in particular, of the reiteration in the Temple Scroll of the Deuteronomic King Law, "thou shalt not put a foreigner over you" (as well as the allied, possible identification in the Temple Scroll of "Bela'" as a circumlocution for Herodians). They had to be present, and so they were, closing and clarifying the whole circle of esoteric allusions at Qumran.

Only the palaeography and archaeology of Qumran have acted as impediments to the formulations and identifications we propose, but we have discussed these at length in *Macabbees*... Where the Habakkuk *Pesher*, in particular, is concerned, palaeography is not an issue, and the only really serious impediment is the archaeology of Qumran. However, as we shall see, this last is neither strong nor secure enough to rule out an otherwise credible textual theory based on the clear sense of the internal data. Spiritually speaking, it is always more comfortable in Qumran studies to think in terms of indistinct or mythological personalities in the far distant past, not *real* people. It is not, however, the task of the historian to be concerned whether or not others will be pleased with the results that are achieved; his charge is simply to detail the implications of the data at his disposal with as much precision as possible.

CHAPTER ONE

BACKGROUNDS

In attempting to set forth a new historical framework in which to view the Dead Sea Scrolls, I have noted the key role played by James the Just in later Qumran sectarian documents, but have not delineated this role in any systematic manner.[1] Since the test of any good hypothesis is to introduce it into the materials under consideration, it would be useful to analyse James' role within the context of one of the most important later sectarian documents, the Habakkuk *Pesher*, and see what results can be achieved. Though there has been substantial discussion over the years concerning the Habakkuk *Pesher*, very little in the way of a consensus has been reached concerning identifications of key personalities, events, and chronology. In addition, there has been a hesitancy in, even an animus against, proposing personalities and events touching upon the historical context and ethos of early Christianity (in the case of this study, the members of Jesus' own family and his purported successors in Palestine).[2] In view of the deep emotions likely to be called forth by such proposals, such a hesitancy is not surprising.

The known details regarding James' life and position are not inconsiderable. In many ways we have more independent documentation concerning him than any other New Testament character, except perhaps Paul. The latter, however, functioned very much in relation to the former, and as he documents his own career, provides, often unwittingly, documentation of James' personality and career.[3] James was a Righteous

---

[1] Cf. *Maccabees, Zadokites, Christians and Qumran: A New Hypothesis of Qumran Origins*, Leiden, 1983, pp. 11, 22, 38, 42, etc.

[2] See, for instance, J. T. Milik, whose remarks are symptomatic: "...although Essenism bore in itself more than one element that in one way or other fertilized the soil from which Christianity was to spring, it is nevertheless evident that the latter religion represents something completely new which can only be adequately explained by the person of Jesus himself"; *Ten Years of Discovery in the Wilderness of Judaea*, London, 1959, p. 43. By way of introduction to this statement, he comments on how "Essene influence" almost took over and submerged "the authentically Christian doctrinal element" in the early Church. But still he sees hardly any similarities between "the generation of the Lord and the first disciples" and "the Essenes"; cf. G. Vermes, *The Dead Sea Scrolls in English*, London, 1962, p. 55: "No properly Judeo-Christian characteristic emerges from the scrolls, and unless we are mistaken the Zealots were scarcely a company of ascetics."

[3] See Ga 1:20-2:13. Paul, for instance, in contrast to the Gospels, places James within the framework of resurrection appearances in 1 Co 15:4ff. Though scholarly opinion has usually tried to downplay this testimony considering it a "Jewish Christian" interpolation, we consider the interpolation in this passage to consist rather of the inaccurate

Teacher-type, and even a casual perusal of the documents at our disposal testifies to the integral connection of the Righteousness-ideal to his person.[4] The letter associated with his name is saturated with what should be called the works/Righteousness approach, as opposed to more Pauline/Hellenistic "free gift of faith"/"grace" doctrines. For the author of James, it is unquestionably Righteousness which (to use the terminology of 1QpHab,viii.2 and xii.14) "saves"; just as it is for the author of 1QpHab and the Qumran Hymns.[5] Filling in from other documents at Qumran and Josephus' description of John the Baptist's *Hesed* and *Zedek* dichotomy, "the Way of Righteousness" is that of the Law and its "acts" or "works" are those of the Law.[6] As the Sermon on

---

"Cephas and the Twelve" (there were only eleven at the time). Vestiges of a resurrection appearance to Jesus' family are, on the contrary, conserved in Luke's Emmaus Road account and confirmed in Jerome's account of the "Hebrew Gospel". When Paul in his introduction of James refers to himself as "specially chosen while still in my mother's womb" (Ga 1:15f.), it is difficult to escape the impression that he does so in competition with the "nazirite from the womb" claims conserved via Hegesippus in all traditions about James; cf. Eusebius, *E.H.* 2.1 and 2.23; Epiphanius, *Haeres.* 29.3 and 78.13; Jerome, *Vir. ill.* 2; etc. The same claim, *i.e.*, being specially chosen while in his mother's womb, is put forth by the author of the Qumran Hymns (presumably the Righteous Teacher himself).

[4] James' superabundant Righteousness, reflected too in his cognomen, is attested to in all the above traditions; see too Gos. Th 12. When the account attributed to Hegesippus refers to James, the epithet "Just One" is applied in place even of his name.

[5] The Habakkuk *Pesher* is acknowledged by all commentators as the palaeographic contemporary of Hymns; cf. Cross, *The Ancient Library of Qumran*, New York, 1961, pp. 198f., nn. 118 and 123, calling 1QpHab "early Herodian". S. Birnbaum, *The Hebrew Scripts*, Leiden, 1971, pp. 38-43, dates 1QpHab "about the middle of the first century"; N. Avigad, "Palaeography of the Dead Sea Scrolls and Related Documents", *Aspects of the Dead Sea Scrolls*, Jerusalem, 1958, pp. 72 and 82, notes the very late palaeographic characteristics of both 1QpHab and Hymns.

[6] *Ant.* 18.5.2 knows John is a "good man" whose "Way" was that of Righteousness (*Zedek*) and Piety (*Hesed*), *i.e.*, Righteousness towards men and Piety towards God. This dichotomy of Righteousness and Piety is the basis of Josephus' descriptions of Essenes in both the *Antiquities* and the *War*. In the Slavonic, we are introduced to a John the Baptist-like "Wild Man" who came in "the Way of the Law" "and called on the Jews to claim their freedom." Mt 21:32 identifies John's "Way" as "the Way of Righteousness", and most accounts make it clear that John was zealous for the Law, since he harangues a member of the Herodian family over an infraction of the law of *zanut* ("fornication") until the latter is forced to put him to death as a public agitator.

At Qumran, where the words used to describe John's mission in the N.T. are actually repeated twice in 1QS,viii-ix, the "Way" terminology and "straightening the Way" imagery is omnipresent. In the first exegesis of Is 40:3 in 1QS,viii.15, the "Way" is identified as "the study of the Law which He commanded by the hand of Moses...and any man...who overtly or covertly transgresses one word of the Law of Moses on any point whatsoever" would be expelled from the community (cf. Ja 2:10ff. in the context of allusion to the "Poor" vs. the "Rich" and the problem of *zanut*: "You see, if a man keeps the whole of the Law, except for one small point at which he fails, he is still guilty of breaking all of it.''); in the second in ix.23, the phraseology "zealous for the Law" actually occurs. In the introduction of the Zadokite Document all these themes, also, come together and "the Way" and its "works" are explicitly identified with those of "the Law".

the Mount puts it in the famous "not one jot or tittle" section: "Unless your Righteousness exceeds that of the scribes and Pharisees, you shall in no wise enter the Kingdom of Heaven."[7]

James, too, is the head of a community, often known euphemistically as "the Jerusalem Church", but for our purposes more accurately described as "the Jerusalem Community", and functions, according to all extant early Church testimony, in something of the manner of an "opposition" high priest. In the light of more recent Qumran evidence suggesting the existence of just such an "opposition" high priesthood basing itself on the Righteousness doctrine and/or the related "Perfection" ideal (which should therefore perhaps be called "Noahic"), one should be wary of dismissing the implications of these notices.[8] Epiphanius and Jerome, probably basing themselves on Hegesippus, are particularly insistent that James went into the Inner Sanctum or Holy of Holies of the Temple either regularly or, from the sense of the text what appears more likely, at least once in his career, there rendering atonement "until the flesh on his knees became as callused as a camel's".[9] Furthermore, Epiphanius insists that he wore the mitre of the High Priest, and all agree that he wore the priestly linen, a right accorded the lower priesthood in the period in which James held sway in Jerusalem.[10]

---

[7] Mt 5:20. The general Righteousness thrust of the Gospel of Matthew should be self-evident; but the Sermon also includes reference to another fundamental theme at Qumran, Perfection. *N.b.*, how the formulations of Ja 2:5ff. actually appear to underlie those of Mt 5:11ff. and present a more authentically "Palestinian" and, therefore in our view, prior rendering of the same materials.

[8] The exegesis of "the Zadokite Covenant" at Qumran is esoteric. It is to be understood in terms of the concept of "Righteousness" that underlies the root-meaning of "Zadok", as much as in terms of any genealogical sense that might be imputed to it. Cf. CD,iv.2ff., where the "sons of Zadok" are defined eschatologically as "those who will stand at the end of days", which is not a genealogical definition at all, but an eschatological one ("stand" carrying with it something of the sense of Ez 37:10). In 1QS,iii.20ff. the phrase "sons of Zadok" is used interchangeably with the usage "sons of *Zedek*" (*i.e.*, sons of Righteousness), which is not the scribal error many commentators take it for. In 1QS,v.2ff., they are unequivocally defined, following the general thrust in Ez 44:7ff., as "the Keepers of the Covenant", *i.e.*, the *Shomrei ha-Brit*. Again, this is not a genealogical definition, but a qualitative one. In discussing baptism, Jesus too is pictured as pointedly mentioning "the commands of all Righteousness" in Mt 3.15; cf. as well *War* 2.1.2/*Ant.* 17.9.1 for the demands of the insurrectionists in 4 B.C.E. for a high priest of "higher purity" and "Piety".

[9] See above n. 3 and n. 13 below.

[10] Epiphanius' testimony in this regard (supported by Jerome) has been dismissed as the grossest exaggeration; cf. H.-J. Schoeps, *Paul: The Theology of the Apostle in the Light of Jewish Religious History*, Philadelphia, 1961, p. 67; however, there can be little doubt that some extraordinary kind of activity is being alluded to in these notices about James. See below, pp. 61ff., for the interesting link-ups between such an atonement (*i.e.*, in our view a "Zadokite" or "Perfectly Righteous" one) and the *blasphemy* trial against James that led to his execution in 62 C.E. Josephus contemptuously calls the right to wear linen (in imitation of James?) won by the lower priesthood shortly after his death, as events moved

One should be chary of dismissing vivid details such as these without carefully considering them. For instance, the Pseudoclementines are particularly forthcoming in telling us that James broke either one or both of his legs in a riot that erupted on the Temple Mount at the instigation of "an Enemy", clearly intended to represent *Paul*—a riot that has as its counterpart in the Book of Acts the events swirling around the attack on "Stephen" (and, one might add, the notice in the *Antiquities* after the stoning of James, about a riot in Jerusalem led by one "Saulus". This same Saulus would also appear to be the intermediary between "the Men of Power, the high priests, the principal of the Pharisees, and all those desirous for peace" and Agrippa, whom Josephus also calls Saulus' "kinsman").[11] James is carried away in a swoon by his supporters to a

towards its stopping of sacrifice on behalf of and rejection of gifts from foreigners, "an innovation"; cf. *Ant.* 20.9.6.

The usage "innovation" or "Innovators" has special significance in both the *War* and the *Antiquities*, especially where the "imposters", "deceivers", and "robbers" are concerned and, in particular, that movement founded by Judas and Sadduk, which Josephus connects with the destruction of the Temple. Josephus employs the same term in *War* 2.17.2 in describing the decision on the part of the lower priest class to stop sacrifice on behalf of Romans and other foreigners which he describes as beginning the uprising, even though he knows perfectly well that from Ezra's time and that of Ezekiel's Zadokite Statement, such xenophobia was common. It has particular relevance vis-a-vis its reversal when discussing Herod in *Ant* 15.10.4; see our discussion of this pivotal notice, below, pp. 78f. and Appendix. These problems over foreigners in the Temple have special relevance, not only where the Pauline "Gentile Mission" was concerned, but also Paul's own difficulties in the Temple.

The "linen" theme also appears in an amusingly distorted manner in Josephus' description of "*Banus*'" wearing "clothing that grew on trees". *Banus* is a contemporary of and difficult to distinguish from James; cf. *Vita 2. N.b.*, the "bathing" theme in Josephus' account of *Banus*, which also recurs in inverted form in the extant testimonies about James. The "bathing" theme with the same characteristic reversal, *i.e.*, "they preferred being unwashed", also recurs in Josephus' description of the Essenes in *War* 2.8.3. Talmudic literature (*Yalqut* Jer 35:12), too, retains a tradition that the sons of the Rechabites were allowed to marry the daughters of the high priests and do service at the altar. By "Rechabites" we understand "Essenes". There were no longer "Rechabites" as such, the euphemism having to do with the abstention by both from anointing with oil, wine, and a propensity towards life-long Naziritism, all themes prominent in extant testimonies about James. In turn, these correspondences link up very well with the notice about Simeon b. Cleophas (James' "cousin") in Eusebius' version of the stoning of James, *i.e.*, that he was a "Rechabite priest" (meaning an "Essene" priest in the Qumran manner).

[11] Rec. 1.70ff. Peter recalls the details of James' injury six weeks later on his first missionary journey to Caesarea when he tells Zacchaeus that James was still limping. Details of this kind are startling in their intimacy and one should hesitate before simply dismissing them as artistic invention. It was H.-J. Schoeps who first drew attention to the interchangeability of the attack on Stephen and the attack on James, both coming at precisely the same point in the narratives of Acts and the Recognitions; cf. *Theologie und Geschichte des Judenchristentums*, Tübingen, 1949, pp. 408-45. For Saulus, see *Ant.* 20.9.4 and *War* 2.17.3. It is interesting that just as Acts misplaces the stoning of "Stephen"; *Antiquities*, where the historiography of Acts and the Recognitions is concerned, misplaces the riot led by "Saulus". Lk 19:1ff., for instance (the first part of the Acts narrative), presents this

location *somewhere outside of Jericho*. It is from here that he sends Peter out on his first missionary journey to confront Simon *Magus*. This confrontation occurs, not in Samaria (as Acts confuses the material with information regarding Simon's Samaritan origins), but in Caesarea, where other material in Josephus shows Simon to have in all likelihood been in the employ of the Herodian family.[12] Detailed accounts such as these are examples of the kind of independent documentation which exists concerning James. While undeniably "lively", it is in the main free of the demonology and fantasizing that often mar parallel New Testament accounts.

We should also pay attention to the motif of a *Yom Kippur* atonement where James' activities on the Temple Mount and possibly in the Holy of Holies are concerned. As we shall see, this has particular relevance where the Habakkuk *Pesher* is concerned.[13] The Letter to the Hebrews also gives us something of the ideological perspective for attributing a "perfectly pure" and Righteous Priesthood to James (language and ideology at the core of parallel "Zadokite" ideologies at Qumran).[14] In addition, where

"Zacchaeus" incident in somewhat inverted form, Now it transpires in "Jericho" (cf. the Pseudoclementines' "Jericho" theme above) and Zacchaeus is a "Rich" *Chief Tax-Collector*, at whose house Jesus stays. Like the *Centurion* in Acts' version of the visit of Simon to Caesarea, he gives generously "to the Poor".

[12] Simon's Samaritan origins in Rec. 1.72ff. become confused with Acts' confrontation between "Philip and Simon" in Samaria in 8:4ff. Acts is usually treated as superior to the Recognitions, but in these sections, anyhow, the sequence in Recognitions (which basically parallels Acts) is preferable. It places the confrontation between the two Simons in Caesarea, where it should be, which links up with the key role played by a similar "Simon" in *Ant.* 20.7.2 in arranging Drusilla's legally reprehensible divorce and remarriage to Felix. This is the same Felix who elsewhere in Acts is described as knowing quite a lot about "the Way". *N.b.* the problem as usual is the *fornication* of *Herodian* rulers (in this case illegal divorce). Here Simon is described as "a Cypriot" by birth; cf. the garbled material about Elymas *Magus* in Acts 13:8 and other individuals described as "Cypriot" in early Christianity. That the Recognitions designates "Simon" as originating from "Gitta" in Samaria need not deter us from appreciating the basic similarities in the traditions in question. *N.b.* the "Gitta"/"*Kittim*" resonance.

[13] Though the portrait in Eusebius and others via Hegesippus is usually taken as referring to habitual activities on James' part, close evaluation of the notices, as we have noted, will reveal that what is being described is only one particular atonement—the unforgettable simile about James' knees becoming like a camel's vividly describing how he spent the whole day on his knees importuning God on behalf of *the people*. In turn, this testimony links up with materials in 1QpHab below, pp. 61ff., about difficulties on *Yom Kippur* between the Righteous Teacher and his nemesis the Wicked Priest.

[14] See, for instance, Heb 2:10, which refers to "the sons (being brought) into glory" and the leader who is "made Perfect through suffering", as well as related notions of adoptionist baptism, i.e., "you are my son; today I have become your father" in 1:5 and 5:6. These last also are connected to being "a priest after the order of Melchizedek"; cf. also 3:1ff., 4:14, and 7:1ff. The suffering motif is alluded to in 1QS,viii.1ff. in the same section as that already called attention to in relation to the evocation of the "Way in the wilderness" symbolism. The notion of "Perfection" is highly developed at Qumran in 1QH and 1QS and goes back to the Genesis characterization of Noah as *ish Zaddik Tamim*.

James' person is concerned, one has the particularly insistent (*i.e.*, all sources consistently and emphatically refer to it) and highly revealing sobriquet of "the Just One", i.e., "the *Zaddik*". This epithet should be viewed against notices in the Pseudoclementines insisting that "the Sadducees" arose in the time of John the Baptist and "withdrew from the community because they thought themselves more Righteous than the others", echoed by notices in both the *Abot de R. Nathan* and Karaite sources about "a split" between "Zadok and Boethus" and the subsequent "withdrawal of the Sadducees". The *sitz-im-leben* of these latter notices must be seen as the "split" between "Sadduk" and Joezer b. Boethus over both the tax issue and the high priesthood around the time of the death of Herod in 4 B.C.E.; and the general implication of these notices when taken together is to make the inception of the "Sadducee" movement virtually indistinguishable from that of what Josephus calls "the fourth philosophy" (*i.e.*, the so-called "Galileans" or "Zealots" founded by "Judas the Galilean" and "Sadduk").[15] One then has the ideological framework for understanding, not only what I believe should be referred to as "the purist Sadducee" movement (as opposed to the Phariseeizing and Romanizing Herodian establishment which might better be termed "Boethusian"), called by most scholars following

---

Though the precise nature of the usage "Melchizedek" at Qumran is under dispute, 1Q Melchizedek does use the phrase "men of the lot of Melchizedek" as another terminological euphemism for "the saved of the last days" and to denote membership in the community of the Elect of Righteousness. The "new priesthood", as it is called in Hebrews, was to be based upon the Perfection ideal, *i.e.*, "holy, innocent, uncontaminated, beyond the influence of Sinners" (often a euphemism for "Gentiles" and more specifically Herodians). These Perfection ideas are also expressed in 1QS,viif. about the Community Council, who are themselves an "offering" unto the Lord and "a sweet fragrance of Righteousness".

[15] Cf. Rec. 1.53f. It is not incurious that these testimonia link up with N.T. notices concerning the birth of the "Zealot" (our "Messianic") movement at the time of the coming of John; Mt 11:12 and Lk 16:16. These related materials in both Talmudic and Karaite sources about a split between "Zadok and Boethus" and a consequent "withdrawal" can be seen as a conflation of two separate "splits" or "withdrawals", one early around the time of Judas Maccabee relating to the appearance of the "Hassidaean" Movement (and not uncoincidentally the "Pharisaic") and a later one relating to the appearance of the "Zealot"/"Messianic" Movement. The clash of "Sadduk" and "Joezer b. Boethus", not only provides the setting for really serious sectarian strife, and consequently Josephus' discussions of the sects in the *War* and the *Antiquities*, but also for his language of "innovations"/"Innovators", which like his "Zealot" vocabulary, has such relevance to the problem of Herodians and other foreigners in the Temple. I discuss the problem of "the new" or "Herodian Sadducees", by which I mean "Boethusians", and "purist Sadducees", following an esoteric interpretation of the Zadokite Covenant, in *Maccabees, Zadokites, Christians and Qumran*. By "purist Sadducees" we must include what presently go under the designations "Essenes", "Zealots", "Jewish Christians", "Zadokites", etc.

Josephus' terminology, "Essenes";[16] but also for understanding, follow-ing the *true* thrust of Ezekiel's *qualitative* distinctions, the esoteric thrust of the "Zadokite" usage as it was developed at Qumran.

It has often been missed that the Zadokite Document's definition of "the sons of Zadok" as "the Elect of Israel" (also identified in the 1QpHab,v.4 with those who "would execute Judgement at the end of time") or "the *Kodesh Shonim*" (*i.e.*, either the *Rishonim* or the *Anshei Kodesh-Tamim*, but in any event equivalent to Ecclesiasticus' *Anshei-Hesed/Zaddikim*), who "justify the Righteous" and "stand at the end of time," is *eschatological*.[17] It is not a normative definition of a priesthood at all; nor is it primarily genealogical. In fact the latter thrust is deliberately broken by the addition of *waw*-constructs in the underlying phraseology of Ez 44:15. This exegesis, strikingly enough, also plays on a second usage, "*nilvim*", which though generally translated as "joined", is ap-plied in Es 9:27 to *Gentiles* attaching themselves to the Jewish community presumably in the manner of converts. We shall see later that a parallel connotation will be discernible in the Nahum *Pesher*, which uses "*nilveh*" and "*nilvu*" relative to those it calls "the Simple Ones of Ephraim", and it will be of the utmost import when finally trying to piece all these trou-bling euphemisms together. It is impossible to over-emphasize such a reference to *Gentile* "God-fearing" auxiliaries attached to the community in associated status. The exegesis in CD,iv clearly carries an esoteric (or qualitative) sense connected with the notion of Righteousness, which is

---

[16] The identification of the sect as "Essenes" is popularly followed by a consensus of scholars, however, in making such an identification, they still have not identified who the "Essenes" were, nor what links they had, if any, with Hassidaeans, Zealots, and the early Christian movement in Palestine. In fact, the terminology "Essene" neither appears as such in the N.T. or Talmud. It is a specialized terminology used only by Philo, Josephus and their dependents. Josephus constantly confuses Essenes and Pharisees, and even mixes up Zealots to a certain extent with Essenes. The identification of Qumran with "the Essenes" simply says something generically about a movement outside the reigning Pharisaic/Sadducean or "Boethusian" establishment of the day, an establishment which was put in place by the Herodian family.

[17] CD.iv,4. The word "stand" here has puzzled most commentators because they usually ignore the eschatological sense of the exegesis. Since the usage specifically relates to "the Last Days", one must realize we are dealing with a resurrection of sorts (*i.e.*, of "the Righteous" dead; the Righteous living according to this ideology "will not taste of death", but go directly into the Kingdom; cf. the use of "stand" with precisely this eschatological sense in Dn 12:13, further expanded in Lam.R,ii.3.6), after which there would be "no more express affiliation with the House of Judah". In this context, therefore, "sons of Zadok" parallels N.T. expressions like "sons of the Resurrection" or its variations. The exegesis actually seems to refer to two classes of these: the *Rishonim* or *Anshei Kodesh-Tamim*, the recipients in a manner of speaking of "the First Covenant", and the Righteous living, or the *Dor ha-Aharon*, the Last or Last Generation, for whom the rededication of "the New Covenant" comes into play.

confirmed too by the presence of material about the "justification of the Righteous" and word-play centering around the "sons of Zadok" usage.

When the implications of these ideologies are combined with the original demand by "the Innovators" in 4 B.C.E. for a high priest of "higher purity"/"greater Piety" and the notices from Heb 4:14f., 7:26ff., 9:11ff., etc. about a Perfect high priest "beyond the reach of Sinners", including a variety of references about "justification", then the reason of a priest/*Zaddik* like James having to make such a *Yom Kippur* atonement at all becomes clearer. Only an atonement by a Righteous priest/*Zaddik* could be considered efficacious in terms of ultimate forgiveness for sin and entrance into the Messianic community/Kingdom of Heaven,[18] and certainly not an atonement made by any members of the Herodian priestly establishment. This establishment and its various families (mostly from the *nouveau riche*), known as "Sadducees" in the New Testament and Josephus, were *inter alia* responsible for the death of James and fanatically opposed by Fourth Philosophy "Innovators" and "Zealot"/"*Sicarii*" sectaries (the pejoratives are Josephus').[19]

Qumran criticizes this establishment over three issues. The first relates to "fornication", a conceptuality playing a prominent role in Acts' description of James' directives to overseas communities and the letter ascribed to his name. By it Qumran specifically denotes *divorce* and *marriage with a niece*. These were forbidden as well, according to Karaite historical reconstruction, by "Zadok", Jesus, and Anan. They were also at the root of the beheading of John the Baptist. The Herod who executed John had married his *niece* Herodias who herself was twice *divorced*—the illegality of which procedure even Josephus feels obliged to remark, as he does her niece Drusilla's subsequent divorce.[20] The second of these three

---

[18] This is paralleled in the presentation of Hebrews. In 2:18 this theme of atoning for human sins is expressed. 6:5ff. exactly parallels material in 1QS,viii-ix; 7.3f. parallels material about adoptionist sonship in Hymns. 5:14 refers to "the doctrine of Righteousness"; 7:26ff. continues the imagery expressing the need for a Righteous atonement. 8:6ff. speaks of the "First Covenant" of the *Rishonim* and brings into play the notion of the New Covenant speaking of "the end of the last age" (9:27), language actually extant at Qumran.

[19] In this period it is edifying to group parties according to their enemies. On this basis, the so-called "Zealots"/"*Sicarii*" have the same antagonists as the "Jerusalem Community" and those responsible for the literature at Qumran. For instance, the high priest, Jonathan, is assassinated in 55 C.E. by a group Josephus chooses to designate as *Sicarii*, but Jonathan is the brother of the high priest, Ananus, who ultimately is responsible (together with Agrippa II) for the stoning of James (according to N.T. accounts his father and uncle were involved too in the death of Jesus). When the revolution enters its extremist or "Jacobin" phase, the various members of the priestly aristocracy, including Ananus, are butchered without mercy; cf. *War* 4.5.2.

[20] CD,iv.15ff., directly following the exegesis of Ez 44:15. See L. Nemoy, "Al-Qirqisani's Account of the Jewish Sects and Christianity", *Hebrew Union College Annual*, 1930, pp. 319-397 for Karaite tradition relating to Zadok's and Jesus' condemnation of

"nets of Belial" is denoted as "Riches". It very definitely is connected with the Herodian priestly establishment and we shall demonstrate this in some detail in our analysis of the Habakkuk *Pesher*'s charge against it of "robbing the Poor" (as the Letter of James describes a parallel sentiment, "a burning fire have you Rich stored up for yourselves"). One also should not fail to remark its reflection in Josephus' description of "the Essenes" and Qumran "Poor" appellations.[21]

The third charge is "profanation of the Sanctuary". We shall see that this last will be one of the charges levelled against the Wicked Priest, *i.e.*, "his Abominations" (*To'evot*) with which "he polluted the Temple" (*yetame' et Mikdash-El*) in 1QpHab,xii.8f. It is certainly reflected too in the Phineas-minded lower priesthood's stopping of sacrifice on behalf of and refusing any longer to accept gifts from Romans and other foreigners (referred to as "an innovation" by Josephus), which triggers the uprising against Rome. It can also be detected to a certain extent in New Testament notices about the antagonism between Paul's "Gentile Mission" and "the Jerusalem Church" and difficulties both Paul and some of his Gentile converts latterly encounter on the Temple Mount. All of these, however tenuously, are connected with the erection of stone-markers in this period warning Gentiles away from the Temple and the general hostility towards the Herodian family, which is only the special case of these currents. This last is very much in evidence in the erection of the wall in the Temple in the late fifties, the controversies surrounding which in our view lead inexorably and directly to the death of James.[22]

---

divorce and marriage with a niece. These practices were widespread among "the Herodians" and Josephus specifically mentions the illegality of the manner in which Herodias *divorced herself* from her husband; *Ant.* 18.5.4. The same combination of factors also circulates about problems relating to Agrippa II's two sisters Drusilla and Bernice, Herodias' nieces, and once again Josephus specifically comments on the illegality of Drusilla's self-divorce; *Ant* 20.7.1ff. *N.b.*, where Bernice is concerned, Josephus makes special mention of "her Riches", her "fornication" (even reputedly with her brother), and how "she forsook...the Jewish religion" after being married to *her uncle* Herod of Chalcis (before she took up with Titus); cf. the same combination of charges in CD,viii.5ff., including "fornication", "Riches", and incest ("approaching near kin for unchastity").

[21] Cf. Ja 5:1ff., *War* 2.8.2, and below, pp. 44f. and 67ff.

[22] The "Temple wall" incident, connected as it is with Agrippa II's Greek banqueting habits in *Ant.* 20.8.11, is crucial. Here, the hostility of the lower priesthood to the Herodian family is patent and this hostility must be connected to a plethora of notices in both Acts and the Pseudoclementines about difficulties on the Temple Mount and the conversion "of a large group of priests" and "zealots" (Acts 6:7 and 21:20). Ultimately, Josephus informs us that "the Innovators" (the same ones who stop sacrifice on behalf of foreigners) succeed in having Agrippa II barred from the whole city (*War* 2.17.1). For the crystallization of Agrippa's relations with the high priest Ananus, see below, n. 32. The whole is paralleled a generation before in the Simon/Agrippa I episode in *Ant.* 19.7.4. Simon, obviously one of the Temple zealots and "the head of an assembly",

Early Church tradition also tells us that James' various titles, *i.e.*, *Zaddik* and *Oblias* ("Protection of the People"/"Bulwark"/"Fortress") were to be found by searching scripture, *i.e.*, that the followers of James followed a style of esoteric exegesis not unsimilar to that pursued by the sectaries at Qumran in analysing the life and character of "the Righteous Teacher".[23] The actual words reported via Hegesippus, who lived within about 100 years of the events in question, were: "And the Prophets declare concerning him", *i.e.*, concerning James and his death. Not surprisingly, the text in question, Is 3:10, is a *zaddik*-passage, and the link is directly drawn between the word "*zaddik*" in the underlying biblical text and the fate and person of the *Moreh-Zedek/Zaddik* James in the exegesis. Every exegetical text at Qumran relating to events concerning the life and person of the Righteous Teacher functions in exactly the same manner. This constitutes persuasive testimony that, not only was Qumran-style exegesis practised by the community descended from James, but that such exegesis was current in this period.

If one looks at the ambiance of the Is 3:10 passage applied to James' death by these early Church sources, one encounters from about Is 1-5 a

---

wishes to bar Agrippa I from the Temple. He is invited to Caesarea to inspect Agrippa I's living arrangements (*i.e.*, the *kashrut* of his house). It is hardly to be doubted that the episode serves as the original model behind the visit of "Simon Peter" to the Roman centurion's house in Caesarea (Cornelius, we are told, "gave generously to Jewish causes"; Acts 10-11; cf. the parallel Lk 19:1ff. above about the "Chief Tax-Collector" Zacchaeus who gives half of what he has *to the Poor*). "Peter" in Acts is nothing but the mirror image of this "Simon" and the episode points the way towards deciphering Acts' "historical method", such as it is. Just as Acts conserves an echo of Peter's ultimate (and unexplained) arrest by Herod (usually taken to be Agrippa I, but just as likely his brother and son-in-law and the "kinsman" of Josephus' "Saulus"—Herod of Chalcis), the "Temple wall" episode under Agrippa II can be identified as the ultimate cause of James' arrest and execution. Agrippa II, working through Ananus, exploits his first opportunity in the aftermath of hi. discomfiture over this issue to deal with the person whom he obviously considers to have been the key to the events we are describing — James the Just. For a further discussion of these matters and their possible reflection in the Temple Scroll, see Appendix.

These real events have their representations in Acts in intimations of confrontations between the apostles and the Jerusalem establishment on the Temple Mount, but they find a more insistent echo in the notices about confrontations on the Temple Mount between Christians and the high priest class in Recognitions which end up in the riot initiated by the "Herodian" Paul. We call Paul "Herodian" because of the intimations he himself makes (cf. Ro 16:11 relating to his "kinsman Herodion"; "the household of Aristobulus" referred to here is, in our view, most likely that of Herod of Chalcis' son by this same name, later King of Lesser Armenia/Cilicia married to that Salome so celebrated in the Gospels and a close collaborator of Titus') and the general religio/political stance of his "Gentile Mission".

[23] See Eusebius, *loc. cit.* At Qumran without exception, where reference is made in a *pesher* to the Righteous Teacher, the biblical text being subjected to exegesis is a *zaddik*-passage; in 1QpHab,i.12 the correspondence is specifically drawn and in CD,i.20 reference to the "soul of the *Zaddik*" actually takes the place of the usual reference to the *Moreh ha-Zedek*.

general tenor of salvation through Righteousness and allusion to the imminent destruction of Jerusalem. The text directly appeals to the *"Beit-Ya'acov"*, James' Hebrew name—repeated three times (which would doubtlessly have appealed to the practitioners of this kind of exegesis) and amid an atmosphere of oncoming armies and imminent destruction precisely analogous to the Habakkuk *Pesher*, intones: "Jerusalem is ruined; Judea is fallen... the Lord is taking away from Jerusalem support of every kind". These last should be compared with the insistence in early Church sources that James' death was in some way connected to the fall of Jerusalem and Paul's description of the central triad of the early Church of "James, Cephas, and John" as "these Pillars". The last in our view incorporates a direct allusion to James' *Zaddik*-nature, which by extension can be seen as a "Zadokite" play (as per the general thrust of Qumran esoteric exegesis and word-play) on the sense of Proverbs' "the *Zaddik* the Foundation of the World".[24] The use of such a style of exegesis explains why the early "Church" felt that the destruction of Jerusalem was inevitable once its "Protection", "Bulwark", or "Pillar" (all allusions having counterparts in the usage of 1QH and 1QS) was removed.

The *Zaddik*-the-Pillar-of-the-World metaphor is also at the root of the allusion to James the Righteous One in the Gospel of Thomas and related materials concerning the disappearance of "Heaven and Earth" in the New Testament "Little Apocalypses".[25] It is the basic thrust behind whatever may be meant by the *Oblias* sobriquet which also attached itself to James' person. Though the precise derivation of the latter is unclear, Eusebius/Hegesippus make it clear that it related to James' "support"/"Protection" activities among the mass of Jewish "Poor" (*Ebionim/'Aniyyim*—"the *Rabbim*" of Qumran/Is 53:11 allusion).[26] With all of this data at our disposal, it would not be difficult to imagine the content of a Qumran-style *pesher* on the first four or five chapters of Isaiah (including an important oracle which has relevance for controversies

---

[24] Cf. Prov 10:25 and its telling elucidation in *Zohar*,i.59b on "Noah", including reference to the "Pillar" terminology applied to James and the central triad in Ga 2:9. The *Zohar* on "Phineas" also employs a facsimile of the "Protection" terminology in relation to Is 53:11's "justification" ideology.

[25] Gos Th 11-12 and Mt 24:35ff., including even the note of pre-existence and the reference to "Noah" amid eschatological evocation of "the flood".

[26] "The People" is a quantity associated at all times and in all testimonies with James' activities. Eusebius/Epiphanius via Hegesippus define *Oblias* as "Protection"/ "Fortress"/"Shield"/or "Strength of the People". Elsewhere James is alluded to as "Bulwark"; cf. *E.H.* 3.7.8. The terminology is paralleled in Hymns in references to its protagonist (presumably the Righteous Teacher himself) as "Shield" (*Ma'oz*), "Wall", "Fortress" (*Migdal*), "a firm Foundation that will not sway", and the general "building" and "Cornerstone" imagery applied to the Council in 1QS,viii.1ff. (which notably includes a central triad).

regarding the Pella-flight tradition: "to flee into the Rocks and the caves"), so exactly parallel in tone and content to the first few chapters of Habakkuk we will analyse.[27]

What then has primarily held scholars back from looking into the implications of these striking parallels about James' life and person and tying them to actual Qumran events and personalities? On the whole this reluctance has centered on the existence of several references in the Habakkuk *Pesher* and elsewhere relating to the fall of Jerusalem and/or the Temple and describing "the Wicked Priest" as actually having "ruled Israel".[28] These allusions, which we shall treat below, have been combined with some very questionable archaeological and palaeographic

---

[27] Cf. "Enter into the rock and hide in the dust . . . for the day of the Lord of Hosts shall be on every one that is proud and lofty . . . and upon all the cedars of Lebanon that are high and lifted up (a favorite image at Qumran and in early Rabbinic literature for the fall of the Temple in 70 C.E.; cf. below, pp. 65f.) and they shall go into the holes of the rocks and into the caves of the earth for fear of the Lord and the glory of his majesty when He arises to shake the earth terribly. On that day a man shall cast his idols of silver and his idols of gold . . . to the moles and to the bats (cf. Ja 5:2: "your wealth is all rotting; your clothes are all eaten up with moths" and similar imagery at the end of the Habakkuk *Pesher*) in order to go into the clefts of the rocks and into the top of the jagged stones". Here, the word is *"sela°im"*, which we take to be the possible source of confused data incorporated into the disputed "Pella" flight tradition of this period; *n.b.* similar "flight" traditions in 4QD[b] and the actual tradition of a "Jericho" flight centering around James' Jerusalem Community in Rec 1.71 above, coinciding with a pronounced rise in Qumran coin distribution during the reign of Agrippa I; cf. as well the parallel flight tradition relating to the *sicarii* after the stoning of their purported leader "Menachem". For the most recent description of the whole controversy, see G. Lüdemann, "The Successors of Pre-70 Jerusalem Christianity: A Critical Evaluation of the Pella-Tradition", *Jewish and Christian Self-Definition*, i, Philadelphia, 1978, pp. 161-73. Lüdemann generally recapitulates G. Strecker; see also S. G. F. Brandon, *Jesus and the Zealots*, New York, 1967, pp. 208ff.

Not only are these first five chapters of Isaiah seemingly addressed to "the House of Jacob" (2:3, 2:5, 2:6, etc.), but their general *sitz-im-leben* parallels that of those sections of Habakkuk already subjected to exegesis at Qumran, including an atmosphere of desolation and the burning of cities with fire (1:7), the use of the fall of the cedars of Lebanon, reference to "the proud and the lofty" imagery above, alluding to the redemption of Zion through "Righteousness" and "faith" (1:26ff., 5:8, 5:16, etc.), combining "fornication" imagery with allusion to "the Judgement of Righteousness" (1:21), evoking the destruction of the city of Sodom in the context of allusions to the removal of the Righteous One (3:9ff.), referring to the saving power of "Knowledge" (*Da°at* at Qumran; 5:14), the original behind CD,ii's "justifying the wicked" and "condemning the Righteous" imagery (5:23ff.), and describing how the "carcasses were mutilated in the midst of the city".

[28] Suggestions about the importance of the "Righteousness" ideal in the delineation of the Zadokite priesthood go all the way back to W. F. Albright (with C. S. Mann), "Qumran and the Essenes: Geography, Chronology, and Identification of the Sect", *BASOR*, Suppl. Studies, 1951, pp. 17ff.; P. Wernberg-Møller, *"Zedek, Zaddik,* and Zadok in the Zadokite Fragments (CDC), the Manual of Discipline (DSD) and the Habakkuk Commentary (SSH)", *V.T.*,iii,1953, pp. 309-15; and R. North, "The Qumran 'Sadducees'", *CBQ*,17,1955, pp. 164-88; but were never developed in any consistent manner. Le Moyne's more recent work, *Les Sadducéans*, Paris, 1972, p. 160 is completely inadequate on this subject.

data, the treatment of which was often affected by the interpretation of such passages and related historical and religious preconceptions, to press the provenance of a large share of Qumran sectarian materials back into the Maccabean age.[29] Most scholars agree that the scrolls were deposited in the caves on or around 68 C.E., but often mistake this date, as we shall see as well below, for the *terminus ad quem* for the deposit of the scrolls in the caves/cessation of Jewish habitation at the site, when it cannot be considered anything but the *terminus a quo* for both of these, *i.e.*, not the latest, but *the earliest* possible date for such deposit and/or Jewish abandonment of the site.[30] The actual *terminus ad quem* for both of these events, however difficult it may be to accept at first, is 136 C.E.

Where the Habakkuk *Pesher* itself is concerned, most scholars acknowledge that it exhibits a substantial number of what are considered

---

[29] I have treated the unscientific use of archaeological and palaeographical data in detail in *Maccabees, Zadokites, Christians and Qumran*. This reference to the Wicked Priest as actually having "ruled Israel" is exploited by commentators to seek out a time when priests were rulers, *i.e.*, the Maccabean period or before, without noting that high priests can always be said to 'have ruled Israel' and that there were subsequent times more in keeping with the plural aspect of the allusion "the last priests of Jerusalem" when priests actually did "rule" Israel, *e.g.* under the high priest Ananus in 62 C.E. and from 66 to 68 C.E. It must be stressed, however, that the reference need not denote a totally independent secular ruler, but simple incumbency in the high priesthood. For Ananus as an independent ruler, see *Vita* 38 and *War* 4.3.9-5.2.

In addition, archaeological and palaeographical reconstructions are set forth on the basis of precisely such preconceptions. The fact that 1QpHab appears to allude either to the fall or imminent fall of the Temple is used to press the *sitz-im-leben* of these references back 100-200 years in time to 37 B.C.E., 63 B.C.E., or before. For an example of the kind of ideological preconceptions we are talking about, see Birnbaum, pp. 69-79, 87, 94, and 103, where he calls the Pharisees, in contradistinction to the "Sadducees", "religious nationalists", uncritically accepts De Vaux's "earthquake" hypothesis in the determination of "pegs" in his palaeographic sequences, and heaps endless abuse on palaeo-Hebrew script, calling it "an artificial revival" and insisting that John Hyrcanus and the Sadducees "would have been the last people to dig out the old script" (since they were not "nationalists"). Cf., as well, Milik in n. 1 above and the general propensity on the part of Qumran scholars to consider the Maccabees suitable candidates for the Wicked Priest, e.g., F. F. Bruce, *Second Thoughts on the Dead Sea Scrolls*, Exeter, 1956, p. 100: ".... in the eyes of the Qumran community every ruler of the Hasmonean dynasty, not being a member of the house of Zadok, held the high-priestly office illegitimately and was *ex officio* a Wicked Priest''; Cross, *The Ancient Library of Qumran*, New York, 1961, pp. 135 and 140, actually calls them "usurpers".

[30] See, for instance, De Vaux, pp. 41 and 138. Note how Birnbaum, p. 27, hardens the import of De Vaux's conclusions considerably: "Archaeological evidence... even enables us to arrive at a precise *terminus ad quem*: the year 68 C.E., when the Romans put an end to the Qumran settlement." Fitzmyer in "The Qumran Scrolls, the Ebionites, and their Literature", *Essays on the Semitic Background of the New Testament*, Missoula, 1974, p. 446, has turned the actual situation completely around: "The latest possible date for the deposit of the manuscripts is the destruction of Qumran in A.D. 68." F. M. Cross, to his credit, realizes that the "absolute *terminus ad quem* for Qumran script types" are the dated documents from the Wadi Murabba'at, though sometimes he behaves as if he doesn't; cf. "The Oldest Manuscripts from Qumran", *SBL*, 1955, p. 163.

"late" palaeographic characteristics, and its being found (like all *pesharim* at Qumran) in a single exemplar and the manner of its deposit also almost certainly identify it as part of the *current* literature of the sect.[31] Despite these factors and the fact that the military procedures depicted in the Habakkuk *Pesher* appear to be those of *Imperial* Rome, most identifications have still involved a wide assortment of Maccabean (or even *pre-Maccabean*) events and characters. This, in turn, entails the somewhat unrealistic proposition that the sectaries were making intense and idiosyncratic scriptural exegeses about persons as antiquated to them as Napoleon or George Washington would seem today to us, and that in addition, they were ignoring 150-250 years of the most vital and significant Palestinian history, the last installments of which were apparently unfolding at that very moment before their eyes. Where the problem of "ruling Israel" is concerned, our candidate for "Wicked Priest", James' nemesis Ananus, did rule Israel virtually in an independent manner on two occasions: the first in 62 C.E., when he took advantage of an interregnum in Roman rule after the death of Festus to dispose of James; and the second, four years later in the first stages of the uprising, before he himself was brutally dispatched by Josephus' "Idumaeans".[32]

The notion of applying the "Wicked Priest" appellation to one or another of the Maccabees—time elements apart—is also hardly convincing. The Maccabees, with the single exception of Alexander Jannaeus, seem to have been on the whole rather "popular" rulers, particularly among apocalyptic and xenophobic nationalists of the kind reflected in the literature at Qumran. Even the Nahum *Pesher*, which appears to refer to Alexander Jannaeus, is not particularly hostile to Alexander, but rather the presumable "Pharisees" he crucifies.[33] Where the reference to

---

[31] If we consider that Cave IV was not inhabited and take it to be either a "library", repository, or *genizah*; then caves like Cave I, which were inhabited, where Habakkuk was found so neatly deposited with a selection of other materials, must contain documents that were actually in use at the time the site was abandoned (whenever this was); cf. R. de Vaux, *Archaeology and the Dead Sea Scrolls*, Oxford, 1973, pp. 44ff., 50ff., 107, etc., for habitation in the caves.

[32] See *Ant.* 20.9.1 for the well-known description of the execution of James. Agrippa II's role in these events has not generally been remarked, since Josephus did not directly call attention to it. An inspection, however, of his appointment and removal of the Boethusian/son of Kanthera high priest, Joseph Cabi (whom the Temple "Zealots" seem to have approved of), leading up to his appointment of Ananus and judicial murder of James, indicates that he took the first opportunity he found after the Temple wall affair to rid himself of James, and that, therefore, he must have blamed James in some manner for his embarrassment by it. *N.b.*, his relations with Ananus appear to have crystallized in the context of previous problems with "Zealot" revolutionaries when Ananus and others had been sent in bonds to Rome in the early fifties and he intervened on Ananus' behalf; *Ant.* 20.7.2f. and *War* 2.12.6.

[33] Milik, for instance, pp. 63f., cannot at all understand Dupont-Sommer's outrage over his suggestion to identify the "heroic and holy" Mattathias with "the man of Belial"

"the last priests of Jerusalem" and the seeming destruction of the Temple in the Habakkuk *Pesher* are concerned, this is an event in progress, not already completed, and from 67/68 onwards with the arrival in Palestine of the main body of Vespasian's troops, the destruction of Jerusalem was a foregone conclusion to any but the most unrealistic observer.[34] Josephus himself realizes as much and quotes Agrippa to the same effect before the uprising even began. In addition, there are two known traditions regarding "opposition" groups in this period implying the same point: 1) the *"Sicarii"* followers of Menachem, the descendant of Judas the *Galilean.* They fled Jerusalem to return to Masada in the aftermath of his *stoning*; 2) the "Jewish Christian" supporters of James the Just who shortly before Vespasian's army encircled Jerusalem are said to have fled in response to the mysterious oracle mentioned above.

Scholars, as we have noted, tend to exploit the above kinds of references to press the *sitz-im-leben* of the Qumran *pesharim* back one hundred, one hundred and fifty, or even two hundred years to a fall of the Temple prior to 70 C.E. In doing so, they often cite this same Nahum *Pesher*, because it actually appears to mention a known foreign ruler—Demetrius, seemingly Alexander Jannaeus' antagonist. However, a careful literary/historical examination of this text will demonstrate it to be retrospective and historiographical in nature and support the opposite conclusion. Though 4QpNah,i.5 explicitly refers to "the Greeks", the reference is to the past and for it "the *Kittim*" (straightforwardly identified in Daniel as *the Romans*) come *after them* and have already appeared.[35] Presumably the sectaries knew their history as well as Josephus (who more than likely spent time with them).[36] "Demetrius" is

---

(whoever such a "man of Belial" might be), and Cross, pp. 158ff., cannot comprehend why Dupont-Sommer would include Aristobulus II in his list of levitical "saviours". I have treated this subject in some detail in *Maccabees, Zadokites, Christians and Qumran.*

[34] The reference in 1QpHab,ix.4ff. is a general one and relates only to the destruction of the Wicked Priest and the last priests of Jerusalem. From 1QpHab,iii to ix, the coming of the *Kittim* is a background event, against which the main concerns of the *pesher*—primarily the struggle between the Teacher and his two antagonists, the Wicked Priest and the Lying Spouter—are enacted.

[35] The stance resembles nothing so much as that of Onias the Just (also "Honi the Circle-Drawer") in *Ant.* 14.2.1, who when brought to condemn the Maccabean partisans of Aristobulus II who took refuge in the city inside the Temple before the Roman assault in 63 B.C.E., refuses, for which reason he is promptly stoned by his presumably Pharisaic interlocutors. Textually, which is to say nothing about palaeography, the Nahum *pesher* is a contemporary of the Habakkuk. Its combination of "Tongue" and "Lying" imagery generically parallels similar usages in Ja 3.5ff.

[36] *Vita* 2 documents Josephus' familiarity with a Qumran-style settlement led by a teacher he cryptically refers to as *"Banus"*, who is a "Bather". This familiarity borders on obsession and is further reflected in his long description of the sects in *War* 2.8.2ff., which is really nothing but a description of "the Essenes", with the other groups added mostly as an afterword. In *Ant.* 18.1.1ff., where Josephus introduces a new character,

mentioned by name because his regime *is* ancient history. Since he is *foreign*, and presumably therefore no longer any threat to those composing the *pesher*, no hesitation is evinced in overtly speaking about him. It is quite another matter regarding the sect's *current* enemies. Here the peculiar and by now familiar exegetical code comes into play because the danger is real and palpable. Nor does the condemnation of crucifixion in i.15 include any condemnation, as we have noted, of "the Furious Young Lion" who perpetrates the outrage. Rather, the text's hostility is aimed at those "Seekers after Smooth Things" he crucifies.[37]

The commentary itself specifies that it relates to the period in which these last, clearly Pharisees, hold sway in Jerusalem, which must be seen as quintessentially the Herodian, *not the Maccabean*. This is reinforced by the general reference to "high priests" or "chief priests" to characterize the principal priestly clans of the *Herodian* period, not the Maccabean. Throughout the former (not before), the Pharisee Party and those "Sadducees" controlled by them were pre-eminent in Jerusalem. Some, as we have noted, even took control under Ananus and Rabban Simeon b. Gamaliel of the first stages of the revolution—Josephus was their commissar in Galilee—attempting thereby to deflect its xenophobic antagonism towards Romans and their Herodian representatives.[38] Quite properly, as it were, the *pesher* blames these "Seekers after Smooth Things" for inviting foreigners like the Herodians, procurators, and the armies of Vespasian and Titus into the country and cooperating with them, not only in the present, but also in the past (the historiographic thrust of the original allusion to Demetrius).[39]

"Sadduk", and is willing to be more forthcoming about the movement initiated by him and Judas the Galilean; he severely curtails his previous description of "the Essenes", adding material previously included under it to his now expanded description of "the fourth philosophy".

[37] The *pesher* itself is indisputably hostile to "the Seekers after Smooth Things". This party, which in the time of Demetrius was sympathetic both to foreign domination and foreign appointment of high priests, is none other than that normally referred to as "Pharisees". As time goes on, one must view the usage as generic, referring to all those advocating peaceful compliance with foreign occupation (*i.e.*, "turning the other cheek" and "rendering unto Caesar what is Caesar's"). In the mid-fifties of the next century, this would include Pauline Christians. In any event, where foreign policy was at issue, Paul is indistinguishable from Pharisaic teachers like Hillel and Shammai, Rabbi Yohanan b. Zacchai, and Simeon b. Shetach of an earlier era—all recommending a policy of accommodation with Romans and other foreigners; cf. Paul in Ro 13:1ff. See below, pp. 32 and 53 for the *War's* reference to how this alignment of those "desirous for peace", when all is lost, *actually invites* the Romans into Jerusalem to suppress the uprising.

[38] See *Vita* 38 and *War* 4.3.9-5.2.

[39] Cf. *Ant.* 13.13.4f. and *War* 1.4.4f. Josephus' knowledge about the period is obviously confused. Not only does he transpose and interchange Sameas and Pollio, but in placing the "Essenes" side-by-side with the "Pharisees", he says the same things about Herod's affection for the one as he does his affection for the other—and for the same

The *Pesher* is not antagonistic to "zealous" Maccabean-style rulers. On the contrary; it is antagonistic to an alliance of "the Seekers after Smooth Things", which we identify with the Herodian Pharisaic/Sadducean establishment, with "those who lead astray"/"lead Many astray" *at the end of days*. In connection with these last allusions, which below we will be able to relate to parodies of the proper "justification" language of Is 53:11, the *pesher* also employs "lying" and "Tongue" imagery as per the Letter of James. In ii.1 it actually makes reference to overseas "messengers" in connection with its "city of blood" allusion, which we will be able to relate to similar allusions in the Habakkuk *Pesher* where the activities of the "lying Spouter" are at issue. Its thrust is to condemn this alliance together with one of the groups it "deceives", which it designates "Ephraim" or "the Simple Ones of Ephraim".[40] In our view, Ananus appertains to an "establishment" party which is part and parcel of this general Pharisaic/Herodian alliance. Though called "Sadducee" in Josephus and the New Testament, it is a latterday caricature of Qumran "Sadducees". For the sake of convenience, it is simpler to refer to it as "Boethusian" after the priest Herod imports from Egypt, as it has

---

reasons; *Ant.* 14.9.3f. and 15.1.1. Continuing the policy of the Pharisees of Demetrius' time, Pollio wins great honor from Herod by advising the citizens of Jerusalem to open their gates to him (Sameas, like "Menachem the Essene", predicted future greatness for Herod when he was a boy). This attitude is hardly distinguishable from that of Yohanan ben Zacchai, who according to ARN 4, when Jerusalem was under siege, shot an arrow into Vespasian's camp to inform him he was "one of the Emperor's friends". All effectively employ the stratagem of predicting future greatness or good fortune for foreign rulers or conquerors in order to toady to their egos. Josephus himself employs the same stratagem and Paul's exceedingly cordial relations with Roman governors and Herodians are detailed in the closing chapters of Acts (*n.b.*, too, the constant reiteration of the theme of "prophets" in N.T. descriptions of early Gentile Christian communities). All the foregoing are important indications of the Pharisaic mentality as we would define it; when Josephus defines opposition leaders like Judas and Sadduk as being in all things like the "Pharisees" except for having an inviolable attachment to liberty, he is, according to this view, very close to the mark.

[40] Cf. Ja 3:5ff. and 4QpNah,ii.8 (also including allusion to "fornication" both as a real circumstance and as imagery; cf. too the allusion "the Simple Ones" tied to this kind of language in iii.7, also referred to in a similarly important context in 1QpHab,xii.4 below). The whole allusion in 4QpNah,ii has particular relevance to the alliance "of all those desirous for peace" signalled in *War* 2.17.3 who oppose the "Innovators" and actually invite the Romans into the city before the revolt could get started in 66 C.E. For more on this connection see below, p. 53. For "the lying Spouter and "the city" he builds upon blood, see 1QpHab,x.9ff. We will in the course of the analysis below of the Habakkuk *Pesher* be able to relate some of these kinds of allusions and the combinations of individuals to which they refer (i.e., "the Men of Violence" and "the Traitors") to Paul and some of his followers or colleagues, particularly renegade "Herodians" or "Idumaeans", like Silas and Niger of Perea, responsible for the death of Ananus. Where the "Ephraim" allusion is concerned in such a context, careful inspection of the Commentary will reveal that it relates like *nilvim* above to non-Jewish believers formerly attached to the community—therefore the signification "Ephraim"; see below pp. 68f.

nothing whatever in common with Qumran's or James' Righteousness-oriented and eschatological exegesis of 'the Zadokite Covenant'.[41]

In such a context it is possible to specify with some precision what these "Smooth Things" were that so exercised the community. They are not so much legal trivialities (though these existed), but rather the broad areas of foreign kingship, foreign appointment of high priests, foreigners and foreign gifts in the Temple, marriage with nieces, divorce, etc., all in one manner or another involving Herodians or those closely associated with them. This anti-Herodian stance is also very much in evidence in the Temple Scroll, which adds the ban on foreign kings and divorce to the Zadokite Document's evocation of the Deuteronomic King Law. Its emphases in later columns on "Abominations" and "pollution" link up with similar concerns in the Habakkuk *Pesher* and Zadokite Document, particularly the latter's charges of not observing proper "separation" procedures in the Temple (probably reflected too, albeit esoterically, in the *"balla͑"*/*"Bela͑"* and "things sacrificed to idols" materials in 11QT,xlvi-xlvii). This antagonism to foreigners and "those seeking accommodation" with them is also reflected in the Zadokite/Zealot Covenant of Nu 25:7ff./Ez 44:7ff. directed respectively against *foreigners in the Community* and *foreigners/backsliders in the Temple* and the "not one jot or tittle" approach to the Law of Mt 5:18/Lu 16:17's Jesus, James in Ja 2:10, and at Qumran in 1QS,viii.22/CD,iv.8. It is reflected, too, in the *debates in the Temple* (refracted in Acts) between *James* and the high priests, as reported in the *Anabathmoi Jacobou* and the Pseudoclementines. These debates parallel and can be none other than those in the Temple between "the Innovators" and the Herodian priestly establishment concerning

---

[41] For detailed enumerations of the various "Herodian" priestly clans, see J. Jeremias, *Jerusalem in the Time of Jesus*, Philadelphia, 1962, pp. 152ff. and 188ff. For Simeon b. Boethus, the eponymous progenitor of the clan, whose daughter married Herod after the latter murdered his Maccabean spouse, see *Ant* 15.9.3 and 17.4.2. For "Simeon b. Kanthera" (a name possibly distorted into Jesus' Talmudic epithet "b. Panthera" and hard to distinguish from the cognomens of two other "sons of Kanthera", Joseph Kami and Joseph Cabi), also a Boethusian, whom Josephus possibly confuses with Simeon b. Boethus and compares to "Simeon the *Zaddik*" two centuries before in the number of his sons doing high priestly service, see *Ant.* 19.6.2ff. Jeremias lists at least seven high priests associated with this family in the first century and connects it, probably correctly, to the famous "Tomb of St. James"/*Bene* Hezir monument. In addition to these, there were several other clans, including "the sons of Ananus" and those of Ananias b. Nebedias. Josephus describes them as "men of little note, whose families were barely those of priests", most notably excepting from this aspersion the Maccabees; *Ant.* 20.10.1. These Herodian Sadducees, for obvious reasons, laid stress on a genealogical interpretation of the Zadokite Covenant as opposed to the Righteousness-oriented one clearly signalled at Qumran, despite the fact that Herod is reported to have jealously destroyed all the genealogical records upon becoming ruler of Palestine; *E.H.* 1.7.13 quoting Julius Africanus.

barring Gentiles (mainly Herodians, but also Romans and other foreigners) and their gifts from the Temple, which are reported so insistently from the 40's to the 60's C.E. by Josephus and trigger the revolt against Rome.

Both the "pollution of the Temple" and "fornication" charges tied to this last are linked in the Zadokite Document to one of "sleeping with women in their periods" (CD,iv.17ff.). Together with its charge of "marrying nieces" (also of concern along with the marital practices of the King generally in the Temple Scroll), this is considered an habitual or customary practice, which, as we shall show in our Appendix, can have meaning only within the perceived sexual mores and marital practices of the *Herodian* family and not those of a *Jewish* priesthood in this period, except derivatively. In line with its theological exigencies (*i.e.*, the *new* Pauline/"Petrine" "Christian" community admitting Gentiles, not barring them), the ideological thrust of these debates is *inverted/reversed* in Acts' portrait of similar debates/problems in the early days of the community in Jerusalem. To make the circle of these allusions complete with regard to such inversions/reversals, one should note the theology in the Pauline corpus (reflected too in the Gospels) of *Jesus as Temple* and the further adumbration of it in Eph 2:2ff. of *equality* in "Christ Jesus", there being no "aliens" or "foreign visitors" (a further ramification is discernible in the parallel represented by Josephus' concern in the *Jewish War* to absolve *the Romans* of guilt in destroying *the Temple* and the contemporary Gospel concern, to absolve them of guilt in destroying *the Christ*).[42]

This parallel of "Jesus" with "Temple", body, community, and community council is perhaps best illustrated by comparing improper "separation"/"pollution of the Temple" materials involving Belial, "Beliar" (*sic*), "things sacrificed to idols", etc. in CD,ivff., 2 Co 6:4ff., and 11QT,xlvi-xlvii. Amid the imagery of "knowing Christ not according to

---

[42] The same puzzling dichotomy of actual Temple and spiritualized sacrifice and atonement is also present at Qumran, most notably in the Temple Scroll and Community Rule. Though the *Anabathmoi Jacobou* portrays James as complaining against "the Temple and the sacrifices" (Epiphanius, *Haeres.* 30.16), it requires only the smallest shift in conceptuality to envision these complaints in terms of the ongoing ones of "the Innovators" against the Herodian establisment over "Temple service" and/or the acceptance of gifts/sacrifices from/on behalf of foreigners/backsliding Jews (Ez 44:9's "uncircumcized in heart and flesh").

Should precise chronological sequencing regarding these approaches be required, this would not be too difficult to provide. When the community were penitents in the wilderness (because of their perception of Temple pollution), spiritualized sacrifice/atonement was the preferred expression of piety; when, in control of the Temple, as at various times in the fifties and sixties, *e.g.*, the building of the high wall to block Agrippa II's view of the sacrifices prior to Ananus' assumption of the high priesthood and James' death and during the last stages of the Uprising, purification of the Temple as per general Temple Scroll parameters (and New Testament portrait) was preferred.

the flesh'', ''the Righteousness of God in Him,'' Truth, ''law-breaking'', ''being Poor but enriching Many,'' and paraphrasing 1QH,ix.35's God as father to all ''the sons of Truth''; 2 Co 6 expounds the charge of ''polluting the Temple of God with idols'' (a variation of the ''Noahic'' proscription on idolatry and James' 'Jerusalem Council' proscription on ''pollutions of the idols'') by asking what ''has Beliar to do with Christ'', ''light with darkness'', and, in effect, ''things sacrificed to idols'' with the body (for 11QT,xlvi, ''Belaʿ'' with ''the Temple'')? Completely parallelling the vocabulary of 11QT,xlvi.10f., the Corinthians text proceeds to invoke ''separating'', ''uncleanness'', ''defiling'', and even ''fearing God'' (connected to the repetition of the ''God-fearing'' theme appellative of Gentiles evoked in 11QT,xlvi.11 in place of Nu 4:20's ''seeing''), ending in evocation of the typical Qumran phraseology ''perfection of Holiness'' (cf. ''*Tamim ha-Kodesh*'' in CD,viii.24ff.). As per the imagery of 1QS,viiif. and Paul's 1 Co 2:13ff. prescription about teaching ''spiritual things spiritually'' (but unlike the exoteric sense of the Temple Scroll), its language is always esoteric; however, there can be no mistaking its relationship to the ''Christ''/''body''/''Temple'', ''Beliar''/''idols''/''Herodians in the Temple'' correspondence.

CHAPTER TWO

HABAKKUK *PESHER* TEXTUAL EXEGESIS

Having set down what some of our ideological and historical parameters ought to be, it now becomes possible to go through the Habakkuk *Pesher* passage by passage and signal its connections to the life and teachings of James the Just. It should be noted, that regardless of one's opinion of their authenticity, the Pseudoclementines *do* place James *with all his community* in the Jericho area (a notice which can hardly be ascribed to historical interpolation). In turn, this notice corresponds to an impressive rise in coin distribution at Qumran during the reign of Agrippa I. In addition, as wise and comfortably safe as the avoidance of making real identifications may be, we know enough about the personalities and events in this period from the variety of sources (even though some of these have been distorted and obscured by tradition) to require scholars to make *meaningful* and *real* historical identifications.

At the outset of the *pesher* we encounter a statement in the underlying Habakkuk text (1:4): "the Wicked encompasses the Righteous". This exactly parallels the sense and signification of the Is 3:10 passage which early Church tradition has retained in the Septuagint rendition, *i.e.*, "Let us remove the Righteous One for he is abhorrent to us", which was applied to the death of James. Both are *"zaddik"* passages and both hinge on contrasting the behaviour of "the Wicked" (almost always identified with the Wicked Priest) with "the Righteous". Both directly apply the usage *"zaddik"* in the underlying text to the subject of their exegesis, James and the Righteous Teacher respectively. In the Habakkuk *Pesher* this connection is even *explicitly* drawn: "the *Zaddik* is the *Moreh ha-Zedek*" (i.12).

Though these early passages of the *pesher* are somewhat fragmentary, their general thrust already relates to "robbing Riches" (i.7), which later will have the specific connotation of "robbing the Poor". This concern is certainly related to the condemnation of the Rich in the Letter of James and Josephus' several notices about the *rich* priests robbing the tithes of "the Poor" so that some even perished for want in the early sixties just prior to James' judicial murder.[1] In addition, one encounters the first

---

[1] Cf. Ja 1:9ff., 2:3ff., 4:7ff. on the humble and the proud (allusions common at Qumran), and 5:1ff. on the final condemnation and destruction of "the Rich", including the phrase "your gold and silver are corroding away" already commented on above. For Qumran, "Riches", "fornication", and "pollution of the Sanctuary"/"idolatry" are

references to "unfaithfulness", quarrelsomeness, and "despising the *Torah* of God" (i.10), with their consonant sense of the perversion of the Righteousness doctrine and the process of justification which the *pesher* will develop in such detail where activities of "the Lying Spouter" are concerned.

This *pesher* has two *bêtes noires*, whose presence along with that of the Teacher's dominate it, and it swings its attention back and forth alternating between them. The first is "the Wicked Priest", the mention of whom is usually tied, as we have seen, to references in the underlying text to *Rasha*ʿ/"Evil", and in connection with whom the Poor are robbed, the Righteous Teacher destroyed, and the city annihilated. The second is "the Man of Lying"/"Pourer out of Lying", who, unlike the Wicked Priest, appears originally to have been a member of the community. He is allied to a group, also seemingly inside the community, referred to as "the House of Absalom". This last euphemism is tied to allusions to "Traitors" (the *Bogdim*) that explain it, *i.e.*, people formerly associated with the community who have "wandered" or been "led astray" and follow the counsel of the Lying Spouter, and to "the Violent Ones"/"Men of Violence" (ʿ*Arizim*), probably coextensive with this House of Absalom/*Bogdim*.

The portrayal of "the Pourer out of Lying" is graphic. In particular, he is said to have "spoken derogatorily about the Law in the midst of the whole congregation", and almost all references to him dwell on his perversion of the Righteous Teacher's proper "justification" activities, *i.e.*, instead of "making Many Righteous", he "leads Many astray" and "wears Many out with worthless service" so that their "ʿ*amal*" (*i.e.*,

---

important themes (as they are in all materials relative to James) and constitute the three characteristic sins of "the sons of Belial", *i.e.*, the ruling hierarchy. The usage, *Ebionim*, is a much underestimated title of self-reference at Qumran and is used in 1QH,v.23 in conjunction even with *Hesed*, *i.e.*, the *Ebionei-Hesed*, "the Poor Ones of Piety". For the insistent theme in the period 55-62 C.E. of robbing the tithes of the "poor" priests, see *Ant.* 20.9.8 and 20.10.2 (*n.b.* the sequence in the latter of the stoning of *James*, the robbing of the poor priests, and the attack on "Stephen" parallels similar sequencing in Acts 6-7). When "the Innovators" finally succeed in stopping sacrifice on behalf of and the acceptance of gifts from Romans and other foreigners at the start of the uprising in 66 C.E., Josephus reports that, not only did they rush to burn the houses of the Herodians and chief priests, but went directly to burn the debt records in order, as he puts it, "to appeal to the people of the *poorer* sort"; *War* 2.16.6 (italics mine). Agrippa II is at this point barred even from entering Jerusalem and their opinion of him and his sister, the fornicating Bernice, is made abundantly clear (*n.b.*, Josephus' report above of her Riches and their incest). Imagery relating both to the problem of fornication (*i.e.*, "prostitutes") and table fellowship ("Sinners", "gluttons", etc.) is turned around in line with the retrospective polemical thrust of the Gospels in order to portray the putative Messiah as being sympathetic to just such classes of people. "Zacchaeus", for instance, in Lu 19:8ff. above is a "Sinful Man" and "Jesus" proclaims the theology of the Pauline mission.

"works" with eschatological effect) will consist of nothing. Together, he and his fellow-traveling "House of Absalom"/"Traitors" and "Violent Ones" are all called "Covenant-Breakers" and "Traitors to the New Covenant", and the animus against them, which focuses on this "Spouter", is so strong that it overwhelms the general background of advancing *Kittim* destroying the land and the debacle being suffered by the people as a whole.[2]

A similar animus can be traced, regardless of palaeographic problems, against an individual or genus of individual in the Community Rule, which includes a blanket condemnation of the kind of easy backsliding path that he has chosen.[3] In iii.3ff. it is specifically stated that: "He shall not be counted among the Righteous, for he has not confirmed the conversion of his life", and his soul is described as detesting "the wise teaching of Righteous Laws". Such an individual or genus of individual is to be barred from the teaching of the Community because he has ploughed "the mud of Wickedness" and returned "defiled" (for purposes of comparison, see Paul's contention in 1 Co 10:23ff. that "for me there are no forbidden things... Do not hesitate to eat anything which is sold in the butcher shops; there is no need to raise questions of conscience"). The passage builds to a climax in the baptismal allusions which follow:

> He shall not be justified (*i.e.*, made *Righteous*) by that which his stubborn heart declares lawful for seeking the Ways of Light, he looks towards Darkness. He shall not be reckoned among the Perfect (*n.b.* this typical Matthaean allusion). He shall neither be purified by atonement, nor cleansed by purifying waters, nor sanctified by (immersion in) seas and rivers, nor washed clean with any ablution. Unclean, unclean shall he be, for as long as he despises the Laws of God (here the word *ma'as* is the same as that of 1QpHab,i.10's "denying the Law" above and 1QpHab,v.11's "rejecting the Law" below), he shall receive no instruction in community doctrine.

In the course of these allusions, one should also note the not insignificant evocation of "the Spirit of Falsehood" and Holy Spirit-type baptism in

---

[2] 1QpHab,ii.1ff.,v.7ff., and vii.2-xiii.4. This usage "*Bogdim*" is found throughout the *pesher* and in the Zadokite Document almost always associated with the Liar/Comedian/Spouter/Windbag. The latter's primary failing appears to have been not following the Law and "removing the boundary markers"; cf.1QpHab,i.3, ii.1ff., v.8ff., x.9ff., and CD,i.12f., viii.4ff., xi.3, etc.; also see 4QpNah,ii-iii. It should also be viewed in connection with allusions in the New Testament to a similar kind of individual and in certain respects, the "Ephraim" usage in the Nahum *Pesher*.

[3] See, for instance, 1QS,vii.13ff. and the extensive references to how to treat such backsliding individuals, who either overtly or covertly transgress the Law; the specific reference to "covert" transgressions is especially important in view of Paul's "Jew to the Jew" and "winning the race" protestations in 1 Co 9:18ff. and consonant behaviour.

iv.26ff. and in v, the stricture to keep away from 'table fellowship' with "the men of Falsehood who walk in the Way of Wickedness", as opposed, of course, to "those who walk in the Way of Perfection" or "Light", which parallels the use of similar terminology in Acts.[4] The text lays down, that "his words are unclean", and further stresses in vii.17ff. that "whoever has slandered the community" or "murmured against the authority of the community shall be expelled and never return". In such a context of "slander" and "murmuring", one should have regard to Paul's "these leaders, these Pillars", "these people who are acknowledged leaders—not that their importance means anything to me" aspersions in Ga 2:6ff. and similar attacks on community leaders in 2 Co 11:23 and in 1 Co 9:5ff. including even "Peter and the brothers of the Lord" (cf. also the reflection of these kinds of difficulties in the symbolic re-enactment of Jn 7-8 with Jesus taking on the persona of Paul).[5]

The Habakkuk *Pesher* presents similar ideas in a more historical context and its exegesis pointedly turns on the allusion to "not believing" in the underlying passage from Hab 1:5:

> This refers to the men, the Traitors together with the Man of Lying (*n. b.* the purposeful linkage of these two categories, later connected to the "House of Absalom" allusion in iv). For they *did not believe* what the Righteous Teacher told them from the mouth of God (note also the allusion to direct revelation where the Righteous Teacher is concerned, an interesting indication of his exalted status). And it also concerns the Traitors to the Laws of God and the New Covenant who *did not believe* in the Covenant of God, but instead profaned his Holy Name (italics mine).

This constant reiteration of the word "believe" here, which in effect became the essence of the new Pauline theological position on salvation, as expressed in Romans, Galatians and Hebrews by reference to Hab 2:4

---

[4] See the "Way" terminology in Acts 16:17, 18:25f., 19:9 and 23, and 24:22ff; for "Light" imagery, see 13:47, 22:6ff., and 26:13ff.

[5] Cf. too similar "murmuring" in Lu 19:7 above. It is noteworthy that the punishment for slandering a companion is denial of *table fellowship*; slandering the community as a whole, expulsion. Paul's murmuring against the "Pillar" apostles or the Jerusalem Church leadership in Ga 2 continues with bitter words about Cephas and is paralleled in Acts 15:38 with unkind remarks directed against "John Mark". In 2 Co 11:5ff., giving vent to his "Tongue", Paul again abuses those people he calls "Archapostles", whom he characterizes as "counterfeit Apostles", "*dishonest workmen* disguised as Apostles of Christ" and "*the Servants of Righteousness*". Then giving full rein to his "Tongue" in alluding to "danger from *so-called brothers*" and boasting "*as brazenly as any of them*" (italics mine); he continues: "Hebrews are they? So am I. Israelites? So am I", which makes it unmistakably clear that his interlocutors were Jews; and alluding to reports of his "cunningness" and stressing that he is not "a Liar" (a stress fairly widespread in the Pauline corpus) and doesn't "lie", he concludes that "there is not a thing these Archapostles have that I do not have as well".

For the use of *ʿezah*—often "Council" at Qumran, but in this instance "counsel" or what I would otherwise translate as "doctrine" or "approach"—see below n. 14.

about to be expounded in this *pesher*,[6] is consistent with the general Qumran predilection for sarcasm, irony, and word-play. Here the point is being strongly drawn by implication, however, that these "faith" doctrines associated with Paul's new "grace" ideas violate the stress in Ezekiel's Zadokite Statement on "keeping the Covenant" (picked up as well, including the emphasis on "keeping" as opposed to "breaking", in the Letter of James), upon which the qualitatively precise definition of the "sons of Zadok" is based in 1QS,v.

The text goes on, confirming its basically eschatological stance, to relate this passage "to the Traitors at the end of days" (the sect here clearly seeing itself living in the "end time" of the Gospels' "this generation not passing away until…"). Using imagery out of the milieu of Ezekiel's Zadokite Statement, these Traitors are identified as "Covenant-Breakers", just as 1QS, following the implied thrust of Ezekiel's Zadokite Statement (particulary Ez 44:3ff.), identifies "the sons of Zadok" as "the Covenant-Keepers", *i.e.*, "the *Shomrei ha-Brit.*"[7] This kind of language and the contrast of "the Keepers" vs. "the Breakers of the Law", not to mention allusion to the Righteousness doctrine, Light, the Lying "Tongue", etc., dominate the first two chapters of the Letter of James as well, culminating in the quotation of the Righteousness commandment of "loving one's neighbor as oneself" and the references to "keeping the whole Law" and "fornication" (2:8-11).

---

[6] In the exegesis of Hab 2:4 below, the Qumran approach turns on the combination of *doing the Law* with restricting the scope of the exegesis only to "Jews" and a stress upon "faith", which otherwise exactly parallels the familiar Pauline formulations.

[7] 1QpHab,ii.1ff. The stress in ii.5 on "Breakers of the Covenant" is the mirror reversal of the definition of "the sons of Zadok" in the Community Rule as "Keepers of the Covenant" (1QS,v.2ff.). When in 44:15, Ezekiel defines "the sons of Zadok", he does so over and against a previous hierarchy that, according to accepted notions of the meaning of the Zadokite priesthood, must also have been "Zadokite". But for Ezekiel (as well as Qumran thereafter), the distinguishing characteristic of a true son of Zadok was qualitative, as per 1QS and Ez 44's "doing their duty in the Sanctuary". When Ezekiel defines just how the previous hierarchy has "broken the Covenant" (the root he uses in 44:7, *P-R-R*, corresponds precisely with this usage in 1QpHab,ii.5), he does so by leveling the charge that they have "admitted aliens uncircumcized in heart and body to frequent my sanctuary and profane my Temple". The "uncircumcized heart" allusion will be used to characterize the Wicked Priest below in x.13. He concludes, "No alien, uncircumcized in heart and body, is to enter my sanctuary, none of these aliens living among the Israelites"—a directive with particular relevance where Paul's difficulties in Jerusalem are concerned and the difficulties of the Herodian family generally with the Temple wall "Zealots". Not unrelated to both of these, as we have already noted above, were the warning stones put up in the Temple in this period warning foreigners on pain of death against illegally entering the Temple; *War* 6.2.4—*pace* Josephus' complaints against the "Innovators" (whom he blames for every disaster) on the issue of stopping sacrifice for and accepting gifts from "foreigners". For more on this subject and its relationship to concerns expressed in both the Zadokite Document and Temple Scroll, see Appendix.

These *Mephirei ha-Brit* (Covenant-Breakers) are described (like "Ephraim" in 4QpNah,ii.3 and ii.8 and "the Simple Ones of Ephraim" in iii.5ff.) as:

> not believing what they heard about all the things that were going to happen in the Last Generation from the Priest (the Righteous Teacher) whose heart God illumined with the understanding to expound all the words of His servants the Prophets to whom God explained all that was going to happen to His people.

Not only are they to be identified with "the Traitors"/"House of Absalom", but at this point also the "Violent Ones" (*ʿArizim*). They were once close enough to the community (before they *betrayed it* by abandoning the Law and going over to "the Liar") *to assist* at the scriptural exegesis sessions of the Righteous Teacher. In addition to his role as scriptural exegete *par excellence* and the connected idea that all the events presently unfolding (*i.e.*, in the present "end time") had already been foretold by prophets like Habakkuk and Isaiah, the above passage evokes the Righteous Teacher's role as "priest", *i.e.*, "high priest".[8] Where James is concerned, we have already discussed above how all early Church sources place particular emphasis on this aspect of his activities.

4QpPs 37 speaks of a group called "the *ʿArizei-Goʾim*" or "the Violent Ones of the Gentiles". These may or may not be coextensive with the *ʿArizim/Bogdim* in the Habakkuk *Pesher*. They were, however, at one time on the same spiritual side of the community, since 4QpPs 37 makes it clear they took vengeance for the death of the Righteous Teacher. In our view they are the force which really triggers the *violent* side of the uprising (therefore the "violent" aspect to the circumlocution) and are to be at least partially identified with Josephus' mysterious "Idumaeans" who take vengeance for the killing of James by brutally dispatching Ananus and quite a few other "collaborators". The "Covenant-Breakers"

---

[8] It is generally conceded that the references to "the Priest" in 1QpHab and 4QpPs 37 carry with them the implied connotation of "the high priest"; in these contexts, he would appear, also, to be identical to "the Righteous Teacher". Such a correspondence allows us to make sense of the testimony to James in early Church tradition as "high priest"; cf. Eusebius, Epiphanius, and Jerome, *loc. cit.*, above. The difficulties that emerge between the Righteous Teacher and the Wicked Priest (evidently the official high priest) over events relating to *Yom Kippur* are referred to below. Such difficulties are not completely irrelevant to the arrest of James on a charge of *blasphemy*. Such a charge primarily relates to pronouncing or encouraging others to pronounce the forbidden name of God, which is precisely the procedure of a *Yom Kippur* atonement. To make extant early Church accounts sensible in this context, it only remains to take the term "Zadokite" in its esoteric sense and to see the atonement reported of James in these sources as involving a "Zadokite" *Yom Kippur* atonement or a properly "Righteous" atonement by a Noahic priest/*Zaddik*; for a fuller treatment, see below pp. 61f.

should include Niger of Perea, "Silas" who was brought up with King Agrippa, possibly "Philip" King Agrippa's bodyguard (whose "daughters" Josephus pointedly mentions in the *Vita*), and Queen Helen's circumcized son Monobazus killed along with John the Essene in the early stages of the uprising. They are what should loosely be referred to as renegade Herodian "Men-of-War" (this last allusion is actually in use in CD,viii) because of the dominance of this element among them (therefore too the "Idumaean" terminology remounting not so much to Herod himself, but more particularly his sometimes subversive brother-in-law and Agrippa's cognate ancestor Costobarus[9]).

What follows is the well known description of the coming of "the *Kittim*" linked to the coming of the Chaldaeans in the underlying text. It is difficult, as we have seen with regard to the Nahum *Pesher*, to escape the conclusion that "the *Kittim*" are the Romans.[10] There has been, of course, much debate on this issue, including detailed analyses of the military tactics of the Romans and Seleucids, but references to their coming "from afar, from the islands of the sea to devour all the peoples like an eagle", marching "across the plain smiting and plundering the cities of the earth", encircling "the strongholds of the people", "tauntingly deriding them", threshing "the earth with their horses and their beasts", "to devour all nations", "in the heat of fury, in searing rage, in scorching anger and with tempestuous mien speaking to all the peoples", "scorning the great and mocking the noble, making sport of kings and princes and ridiculing any large host" can hardly be thought of as relating to the Seleucids, attempts to portray them in this manner notwithstanding. The note about "sacrificing to their standards and worshipping their weapons" in a continuation of this description in vi.3ff. below, also (as has been argued) certainly reflects the practices of Imperial, not Republican, Rome.

Nor must such a reference reflect any specific sacrifice made by the Romans. The reference is a general one, and certainly does not entail the sacrifice the Romans made on the Temple Mount at the end of the war (the only one Josephus describes) as it is usually taken as doing. The Romans must have made quite a few as they made their bloody way down from Galilee, and Josephus describes the consternation engendered in Jerusalem by the reduction of a series of Galilean strongholds: Gadara, Jotapata, Taricheae, Gamala, etc., all the time making continual

---

[9] For the connection of "Saulus" to other seeming descendants of this "Costobarus", see *War* 2.17.3. Costobarus is the real "Idumaean" in these genealogies, Herod's origins being somewhat more difficult to trace. See also n. 44, p. 64 below.

[10] 1QpHab,ii.12 and 4QpNah,i.5; cf. Dn 11:30.

reference to the "Innovators" as the principal element disturbing the commonweal in Galilee.[11]

It cannot be stressed too often that for the *pesher* the Roman conquest is an event *in progress*, not finished. The conclusion some draw from such allusions, in particular one to the destruction of the Temple and/or Jerusalem, that the *pesher* either would have had to be written after the events of 70 C.E. (which is *not* archaeologically speaking *impossible*) or barring this, a century or two earlier, is therefore *not proven*. The conquest and the destruction it entailed, as we have seen, were a foregone conclusion as early as 67 or 68 C.E., and, as we have also noted, Josephus and quite a few others were aware of this, as was James' nemesis Ananus[12]. On the contrary, if the notice in iv.10ff. to "the rulers of the *Kittim* in conference in their guilt-ridden house replacing their rulers one after the other and each coming in turn to destroy the earth" refers to 'the year of the three Emperors', as it is sometimes taken as doing, then one has a *solid textual* measure for dating the commentary. Again, however, this passage need not refer to a given year such as 68 C.E., but to Roman emperors from Caligula to Vespasian. Whatever one's conclusion concerning any or all of these matters, it is clear that the *sitz-im-leben* of the *pesher* has little historical relation to any context earlier than this.

Having described these background disasters, the *pesher* now returns to its favorite topic, the salvation of those who "keep the Covenant"/"the Commandments", and its preoccupation with internecine strife. It contends, somewhat poignantly, that despite the horrors that were transpiring, "God will not annihilate his people at the hands of the Gentiles" (v.3; the use of *Go'im* here as opposed to *Kittim* is not insignificant as it relates to the *pesher*'s concern with "Gentiles" generally, in particular that "Judgement" which will be pronounced on them, including the Pourer out of Lying and those of his persuasion, as well as Jewish backsliders in x and xiif.). It insists rather that "God *will execute Judgement on all the Gentiles by the hands of His Elect*, in connection with which chastisement all the Wicked Ones among his own people who kept the Com-

---

[11] 1QpHab,vi.3ff. One such sacrifice is, of course, recorded in *War* 6.6.1, but there is absolutely no proof that this was the one hinted at in the commentary; on the contrary, the notice there is general, not specific. *N.b.* in *War* 3.8.9-10 Josephus gives a long description of the towns around "the Lake of Gennesareth", the locale of the most serious "seditious" activities, in particular naming one "Jesus the son of Shaphat" as "the principal head of the robber band".

[12] *War* 2.16.4f. and 4.5.2. It is certainly curious that Josephus in the latter notice records of Ananus (whom he scornfully dismisses as corrupt and intemperate in *Vita* and *Ant.*) precisely what early Church tradition insists he said of James in the extant copies of Josephus' works, *i.e.*, that the fall of Jerusalem was directly related to his death and that the Roman armies appeared immediately following his removal; cf. *E.H.* 2.23.18ff. and Origen, *contra Celsum* 1.47 and 2.13 and *Comm. in Matt.* 10.17.

mandments only when convenient will also be condemned'' (here the employment of the allusion ''the Wicked of His People''—*Rishi͑ei-͑amo*—is important, for it includes Jewish backsliders of the genre of the pro-Herodian ''Wicked Priest''). There can be no doubt at either the 'nationalism' of this insistence; nor the *zeal* of its apocalyptic—*i.e.*, these are not 'peaceful Essenes'; nor can the era be anything resembling the Seleucid one.

Where backsliding/turncoat Jews are at issue, the stress in the exegesis on the theme of ''keeping'' is important. It should be noted that CD,iv's exegesis of the Zadokite Covenant identifies ''the sons of Zadok'' *as* ''the Elect of Israel'' (''who would stand at the end of days''—*i.e.*, those who would ''execute Judgement on all the Gentiles'' and backsliding Jews above). The whole assertion is followed, not incidentally, by an allusion to that same *''zanut''* (fornication—v.7f.) so important to the Zadokite Document, the Letter of James, and deadly difficulties with the Herodian family generally.[13] Here it is ''the Elect'' who ''have not lusted after their eyes'' (*i.e.*, married nieces or divorced illegally), and the allusion to ''the era of Wickedness'' is quite simply the Herodian age. One should also note the use of *zanut* imagery along with ''lying lips'' and ''Tongue'' allusions in the ''selling *zanut* to the Gentiles'' and ''leading Ephraim astray'' section of 4QpNah,ii.7ff.

This brings us in the text to a dramatic confrontation between ''the Liar'' and those of his ''persuasion'' and the Righteous Teacher, the importance of which should not be underestimated. That the confrontation is *verbal*, though it could be otherwise, is given some confirmation by the reference to treachery in the underlying text, interpreted to relate to factional strife within the community, and the usage *ma͗as* which dominates the actual exegesis, *i.e.*, ''despising'' or ''speaking derogatorily about the Law'' or ''Covenant'' as in 1QpHab,i.10 above. Since once again it is the Righteous Teacher who is the subject of the exegesis, the signification being played upon in the underlying text to construct the exegesis is ''*zaddik*''. As so often elsewhere, it is connected with *Rasha͑*, *i.e.*, the Righteous vs. the Evil Ones. Here the much-vexed turn of phrase ''the House of Absalom and the men of their persuasion'' in the exegesis is tied definitively to ''*Bogdim*'' in the underlying text, thus confirming the figurative sense of the ''Absalom'' ascription (with the possible additional imputation of treachery within the Messianic family itself).

---

[13] For an excellent glimpse of the importance of *zanut* at Qumran, one should have regard to 1QS,iv.9ff.'s abuse of its genre of ''lying'' nemesis who follows ''the Ways of Nothingness''—cf. 1QpHab,x.9ff.'s ''the City of Nothingness'' built by the Liar, etc. below pp. 53ff.—who has ''a Spirit of fornication'', ''lying'', and ''whoredom'', ''zeal for lustfulness'', ''works of nothingness'', and ''a Tongue full of insults''.

Already linked earlier in the text to "the Covenant-Breakers", "the Man of Lying", and the ʿ*Arizim* (possibly, but not necessarily, linked to the ʿ*Arizei-Goʾim* in 4QpPs 37), the House of Absalom ("*Bogdim*") "remained silent when the Righteous Teacher was being abused (*i.e.*, "verbally abused") and did not help him (since we are in an assembly of some kind involving "the whole community"—possibly of the Pentecost variety in Acts—the meaning is actually "speak up") against the Man of Lying *who rejected the Law in the midst of their entire community*" (italics mine).[14]

It should be clear that this confrontation is *internal* and that the "Traitors" play some role *within the community* or as adjuncts to it (therefore the "treachery" imputation). For 1QpHab,x.9ff. below, "the Pourer Out of Lying"/"Spouter" (*Mattif ha-Cazav*—identical with "the Man of Lying" and playing as well on the baptismal imagery of CD,i.14ff.'s "pouring the waters of lying") is also someone inside the community, not outside it. For precisely this kind of ideological dispute, see Ga 2:11ff., where Paul does speak "derogatorily about the Law" (as he probably did in Jerusalem earlier when he went up to put the version of the Gospel as he taught it to the Gentiles fearing that the course he "was adopting or had already adopted would be in vain"), in the process verbally abusing one of the community's most respected leaders and blaming his problems on personal difficulties with James and "the group which insisted on circumcision" in Jerusalem. "Circumcision" was 'in the air' in "Asia" in this period (a primary venue of Paul's missionary activities), as its cruciality in the marriages of Herodian princesses in Cilicia, Emesa, and Commagene and the conversion of Queen Helen's husband or son in Adiabene attest. 1QS,viii.20ff. gives a picture of the likely Qumran reaction to such remonstrations: "Any man who enters the Council of Holiness, walking in the way of Perfection as commanded by God, and, whether overtly or covertly transgresses one word of the Lord of Moses on any point whatsoever (cf. the "not one jot or tittle" allusions in the N.T.), shall be expelled from the Council of the Community and return no more. No man of Holiness shall be associated with him in monetary dealings or in approach *on any matter whatsoever*."

This last by his own testimony is precisely how Paul is treated after the confrontation in Antioch: "The other Jews joined him (Cephas) in this pretense and even Barnabas felt obliged to copy their behaviour". In fact, according to the presentation of Acts 15:39, Barnabas, too, parts

---

[14] 1QpHab,v.7ff. As opposed to Roth and Driver, "the House of Absalom" is to be taken figuratively as implying *betrayal* or *treachery*. The word "ʿ*azatam*" here is used to signify "their persuasion" (not "their Council").

company with Paul, *i.e.*, "after a violent quarrel, they (Paul and Barnabas) parted company and Barnabas sailed off with Mark to Cyprus". From this point Barnabas and the Jewish apostles have little more to do with Paul, and despite a few isolated notices in the corpus attributed to him, few, if any, *Jewish* apostles or *Jews* (as opposed to what we would call "Herodians") appear willing to associate themselves with his "mission". J. Teicher in the early history of Qumran research developed the position that we are presenting to a certain extent (inspired by G. Margoliouth's early identification of the Cairo *Genizah* Zadokite Document as "Jewish Christian"); however, by ignoring James and dwelling too closely on purported difficulties between *Paul and Jesus*, he vitiated the historicity of his approach and put the entire perspective into ill repute. Since his historical grasp was so unincisive, he did not make sense out of any of the "Men of Violence"/"Men-of-War"/"Traitors" terminologies either.

Another, more physical, attack by Paul on James is reported in the Pseudoclementines. On the whole, however, this notice in the Habakkuk *Pesher* must be taken as parallelling a more ideological attack which probably occurred in the context of events relating to the so-called "Jerusalem Council" reported in Acts. We would consider Paul's view of similar events in Ga 2:1-10 to be a more accurate presentation of the progression of these events (if not of how they were perceived by "the Jerusalem Church"). The characterization of "the Man of Lying" as "repudiating" or "speaking derogatorily about the Law in the midst of their entire community" in v.11 also receives, through the word "*ma'as*", generic reinforcement in the Community Rule and the Zadokite Document. The underlying text in question, "the Wicked confounds one more Righteous than he", precisely parallels the sense of other *zaddik* texts applied to the Righteous Teacher and James. "The Wicked" in v.9 is *not* interpreted in terms of "the Wicked Priest", who emerges later in the *pesher* in the context of chronologically later, more political, squabbling when the destruction of Jerusalem is imminent. Rather, it is specifically applied to "the Man of Lying", whom along with his fellow travelers "the Traitors" and *'Arizim*, the *pesher* has already characterized as being privy to, but "not believing in", the esoteric scriptural exegeses of "the Priest"/Righteous Teacher. The whole constitutes a perfect representation (including even the incessant theme of verbal derogation of the community leadership and the earlier ironic allusion to Pauline "belief" doctrines) of the split between Paul with his more antinomian "free gift of faith"/"descent of the Holy Spirit" approach and those following the *Zaddik* James insisting both on "works of the Law" and its concomitant in "Perfect Righteousness (*Tom-Derech* or *Tamim-Derech* at Qumran).[15]

"The House of Absalom" can be, therefore, definitively identified as ideological "Traitors" within the movement who are willing to go along with the antinomian position of "the Man of Lying"—in our view also referred to by the usage "the Enemy" in the Pseudoclementines. In this, they are connected with the "*'Arizim*", *i.e.*, renegade "Herodians" and those "Men of War" who are reported to have gone over to "the Liar" in the Zadokite Document (viii.37; cf, also the use of "*ma'as*"/rejecting, "going astray", "the House of the *Torah*", "faith", "the New Covenant", etc. in this passage). They are not so different from the more general "Ephraim"/"City of Ephraim"/"Simple Ones of Ephraim" in the Nahum *Pesher* linking up with "city of blood"/"city built upon blood" allusions in it and 1QpHab,x which we shall presently elucidate below.

The drama of this moment should not be lost on any student of early Church history, and its religio-historical implications are far-reaching. If our interpretation is correct, we have in it nothing less than a version of that meeting or confrontation, which is referred to by all commentators as "the Jerusalem Council"—a more likely euphemism in the present context would be "the Assembly of the Jerusalem Community."[16] Its

---

[15] It usually goes unremarked that the usage *ma'asim* or one of its several variations, *ma'asei/ma'aseihem* (which translate into what we would term "works"), completely pervades Qumran usage. So widespread is the usage, beginning in the introduction of the Zadokite Document (CD,i.10) and often in conjunction with its ideological opposite *ma'asei-Sheker* and *ma'asei-niddah* associated with the Liar ("Lying works" and "works of Uncleanness"—the "*niddah*" usage also occurs in relation to "pollution of the Temple" charges in viii.13) and the men of his persuasion, that cataloguing it is beyond the scope of this study. In this section of the Habakkuk *Pesher* one has to do with a further variation of the usage, the *'Osei ha-Torah* or "Doers of the Torah" (1QpHab,vii.11 and viii.1; cf. Ja 1:22ff. also alluding to "Doers"). A significant ideological counterpart of this usage is the term, *'amal*, which also has the signification of "works", but "works" in the most soteriologically efficacious sense—in this case "suffering works" or "travail". Not only is the usage *'amal* crucial to the eschatological exegesis Hab 2:4 which is to follow, it is repeated with opposite ideological signification at the end of the *pesher* in relation to the activities of the Liar. It, too, is based on terminology in the all-important Is 53:11f. prooftext (also a *zaddik*-passage).

The *Derech*/"Way" terminology is rarely discussed in any detail in Qumran scholarship. The terminology has strong connections with exegetical usages surrounding the mission and activities of John the Baptist and is at the root of allied Qumran usages centering around the root *Y-Sh-R*—meaning "straightening"/"Upright". The almost total addiction at Qumran to the "Perfection" terminology connected to it, a usage well-known in the N.T., is also underestimated. For *Tom-Derech* or *Tamim/Tamimei-Derech*, see, for instance, 1QS,i.12ff., v.24, viii.10ff., ix.6ff., x.22ff., xi.2ff., etc. and cf. Mt 5:48's "be Perfect as your Father in Heaven is Perfect" and Mt 19:21, Acts 22:3, 24:22, Ga 3:3., etc.

[16] The allusion "Jerusalem Council" has grown up surrounding the confrontation between Paul and the "Jerusalem Church" leadership, concerning both the advisability and

point-of-view, however, is "internal", or "Palestinian"/"Jewish Christian", *i.e.*, that of "the Keepers of the Law" as opposed to those "Law-Breakers" breaking it and those advocating the opposite policy within the early "Church". As we have noted, too, its connection with Paul's Ga 2:11-14 confrontation with and charges against Peter in Antioch is intrinsic. One should not be too astonished at our linking this seemingly innocuous notice in the Habakkuk *Pesher* (not innocuous in terms of the literary devices of compression, ironic understatement, and parody practised at Qumran) with the famous "Jerusalem Council". In our view it *is* the actual confrontation as viewed from the point-of-view of Jerusalem and the supporters of James; not *vice versa*. That this confrontation made a very lasting impression on the members of the early community is confirmed, not only from Acts' one-sided portrayal of it, but also in Paul's version of these events in Ga 2. Along with some other matters of equal

---

terms of reference of "the Gentile Mission"; cf. Ga 2 and Acts 15. Certainly 1QS,viii.1ff. refers to a central "Council" of the Community which appears made up of twelve members, of whom "three are priests" or to which "three priests are added" (the sense here is tantalizingly obscure, but the dichotomy of priestly and Israelite imagery which follows suggests "the three" are part and parcel of "the twelve," not added to it as majority scholarship generally thinks). It is in relation to and following the delineation of this council that the text evokes the imagery of "atonement by suffering", and it is this Council which is referred to as "a House of Perfection and Truth for Israel" and "a Holy of Holies for Aaron" (*n.b.*, the "Israelite"/"priestly" dichotomy referring to one and the same council). In a further extension of this Pauline-type "spiritualized" Temple and atonement imagery, the Council is referred to as "a sin offering" and "a sweet fragrance". All of this imagery is evoked in relation to the dual citation of "the Way in the wilderness" passage which is used, as already noted, to epitomize the activities of the community.

The Hebrew word for "council", *'ezah*, is also used, as we have seen in n. 14, to designate "teaching", "approach", or "persuasion", as, for instance, "the approach" or "persuasion of the Liar". The usage "Jerusalem Council" has something to do in Acts with an "Assembly", which appears to convene itself in Jerusalem at the time of Pentecost (a time of convocation also important for 4QD[b]) probably in reaffirmation of the traditional notion of the descent of the Law associated with this festival. In Acts 2:1ff. this "descent of the Law" is parodied in terms of a more Paulinized "Holy Spirit", which descends together with its Gentile Mission accoutrements of "speaking in tongues" and doing "mighty works", by which is intended cures, exorcisms, and the like, not "works of the Law" as in James and at Qumran. Another notice about an opposition "assembly" in Jerusalem appears in *Ant.* 19.7.4 in connection with that "Simon", who wishes to exclude Agrippa I from the Temple as a "foreigner" and his visit to *Caesarea* to inspect the latter's living arrangements (*i.e.*, his household *kashrut*). It should be increasingly clear to the reader that this, in fact, is the authentic and demythologized "Simon" as opposed to his ideological and diametrically opposite mirror image in Acts. Simon in Acts, instead of inspecting the *kashrut* of Agrippa I's household as the Simon in the *Antiquities*, rather visits the household of the Roman centurion Cornelius in Caesarea who is described as "giving generously to Jewish causes", a notice which more appropriately suits Agrippa I. He is prepared for this "visit" by a special vision via the always useful "Holy Spirit" mechanism repealing, it would appear, for all of time the normal Jewish dietary regulations. Cf. the parallel here of Jesus' visit to the Rich "Zacchaeus" in Lu 19, developing into a parable about a king not unlike Agrippa (or his grandfather Herod).

import relating to "the Lying Spouter and those of his persuasion", it has made an equally indelible, if ideologically opposite, impression on the authors of the Habakkuk *Pesher*.

Habakkuk was, of course, a very important prophet for the sectaries, as he was for the authors of 2 Macc. One should also note in this regard that Habakkuk, like Phineas, Elijah, Onias the Just (Honi the Circle-Drawer), Hanan the Hidden, and James himself, was a primordial rain-maker. Eschatological notions and the Righteousness ideal associated with rain and rain-making go back to the soteriological activities of the first *Zaddik* Noah. The *ARN* associates "the bringing of rain" with proper (*i.e.*, "Zadokite") Temple service; drought with its cessation; and rain-making and its associated mechanism of circle-drawing were important attributes in the determination of the true *Zaddik* and eschatological high priest. Rain-making and "Messianic" rain imagery are integrally related, too, to the parallel imagery of "the Son of Man coming on the clouds of Heaven", and in a sense, all three imageries are combined in the last two chapters of the letter conserved under James' name. The Son of Man coming on the clouds of Heaven, according to Eusebius/Hegesippus' testimony, also comprised the essence of James' Messianic proclamation in the Temple before his death, and, once again, all are to a certain extent invoked in combination with the exegesis of the Messianic "Star" prophecy in the Qumran War Scroll.[17]

The Habakkuk *Pesher* is impressed, not surprisingly, with God's having commanded Habakkuk to "write down" his vision concerning what

---

[17] For Habakkuk as rain-maker, see the whole narrative relating to Honi and his descendants in b. Ta᷾an 23aff. That James, too, functioned as a rain-maker is confirmed by Epiphanius in *Haeres*. 78.14 (the notice is too original to be simply dismissed as spurious). As such, he is a contemporary of and exhibits suspiciously similar characteristics to another "rain-making" grandson of Honi, Abba Hilkiah. Rabbinic literature unerringly designates Phineas as a rain-maker, anticipating Elijah in this activity, his successor in the *redivivus* tradition, and depicts similar activities on the part of Hanan *ha-Nehba*, another grandson of Honi, who is often identified with John the Baptist.

That the coming of the Messiah in the company of the host of Heaven "on the clouds" was associated as well with eschatological "rain" imagery is confirmed in 1QM,xi.10ff. It evokes this imagery in connection with its exegesis of Nu 24:17, which it purposefully expounds in terms of Daniel's portrait of "the Son of Man coming on the clouds of Heaven"—the favorite simile regarding the hope for a Messianic return. This hope is also expressed following James' condemnation of the Rich (whom he blames for the crucifixion of "the Just One") in connection with his counsel of "patience... until the Lord's coming" in Ja 5:7ff. Here, James again ties the allusion to eschatological "rain" imagery and even evokes Elijah, making the connection between the various allusions and imageries unmistakably clear. In fact, the proclamation of just such a Messianic return forms the substance of James' speech on the Temple stairs at Passover, alluded to in all sources, which either forms the background of the riot on the Temple Mount or events culminating in his judicial murder; cf. as well Paul in 1 Thess 3:13. Jude in 1:12ff. actually explains the imagery.

would happen in "the last generation" (2:1f.). However, for it God did not make known to Habakkuk "when the time of the end would be completed." Rather this information was vouchsafed to the Righteous Teacher in his role as scriptural exegete *par excellence* "to whom God made known all the mysteries of the words of His servants the Prophets" (vii.4ff.). Having said this, the *pesher* then proceeds to interpret Hab 2:3 (which itself leads to the all-important citation from Hab 2:4: "the Righteous shall live by his faith") as the scriptural warrant for what in other vocabularies goes by the name of "the delay of the *Parousia*". Nothing could better confirm the overall eschatological thrust of the Habakkuk *Pesher*, evinced whenever notions relating to "the End" or "the Last" are discussed, than this exegesis of Hab 2:3. The declaration that "there shall be yet another vision concerning the End" (which includes not insignificantly an aside about "not lying"—cf. Paul in Ro 9:1, 2 Co 11:31; Ga 1:20 and *par contra* Ja 3:14) is expounded to mean that "the final moment would be protracted beyond anything which the Prophets foretold". The very matter-of-factness of this statement is possibly the reason for its having been generally overlooked by most scholarship. Not only do we have in it the explanation (based on the scriptural warrant of Hab 2:3, introducing the all-important materials in 2:4) of why "the End", also so clearly expected in the New Testament, was not going to materialize in this generation, but by implication, too, that such an expectation was part and parcel of the Messianic fervor surrounding the uprising. Where the latter was concerned, such a delay in the institution of "the Messianic Kingdom" was not suprising in view of its subversion by people like Ananus, Josephus, Agrippa II, and Philo's renegade nephew Tiberius Alexander, responsible for the death of not a few "Messianic" leaders and Titus' actual military commander at Jerusalem.

 Commenting with perhaps more irony than even it intended, "for the mysteries of God are astounding", the *pesher* explains the next sentence: "If it tarries, wait for it, for it shall surely come and shall not be late", in terms of how the faithful should behave in the face of such a 'delay'. In so doing, it makes its first allusion to "the Doers of the Law" (*ʿOsei ha-Torah*), which will be one of the cornerstones of its exegesis of 2:4 to follow (as well as its description of "the Simple Ones of Judah" who will be the beneficiaries of the justifying activities of the Community Council and destroyed by the Wicked Priest's "acts of Abominations" at the end of the *pesher*) *viz.*: "The Men of Truth who are *Doers of Torah*" are not to "slacken from the service of Truth though the final age is prolonged". Allusions to "Truth" are common at Qumran from "the sons of Truth" in 1QS,iv.5 to "the sons of your Truth" in Hymns and to a certain extent may be viewed in the context of those "lying" allusions predicated of "the Liar".[18] The *pesher* concludes on an optimistic, if mysterious, note: "all the times appointed by God necessarily come as He has determined them according to the mysteries of His Wisdom".

This expression of the most exalted theological faith and unwillingness to despair even in the face of overwhelming tragedy, not to mention the pathos of it at this particular historical moment, has also been systematically overlooked in the dating of this *pesher*. The "doing" or "Doers of the *Torah*" tied to it are the analogue of such important expressions elsewhere in the Qumran corpus like *Shomrei ha-Brit*/"Keepers of the Covenant" or *Nozrei-Brito*/"Keepers of his Covenant". The definition of "the sons of Zadok", their most perfect embodiment, turns in the Zadokite Document on an allusion to "doing"/"works" (both based on the Hebrew root ʿ-*S-H*), in particular, "doing the precise sense of the Law", and the identity of the Habakkuk *Pesher*'s "Law-Doers" and the Zadokite Document's "sons of Zadok" is, therefore, intrinsic.[19] CD,iv's definition also turns on the allusion to "justifying the Righteous and condemning the Wicked", embodying the "*yazdik-zaddik*" or "justification" ideology of Is 53:11, which itself has very real connections with

---

[18] *Emet* is another basic notation at Qumran, which along with usages like *Daʿat*, *ʿamal/maʿaseh*, *Zedek*, *Hesed*, and *Tom*, must be exhaustively catalogued. "Men of Truth" (1QH,xiv.2) and "sons of Your Truth" (1QH,vii.29f.—*n.b.* God here is the "father of all the sons of Truth"; ix.35; x.25; xi.11) are parallel notations of self-designation in use by the sect, like "sons of Righteousness", "sons of *Hesed*", "sons of Light", and "the Perfect of the Way"; cf. 1QS,i.5f., *Brit-Emet* and *Zedek*; iii.6, *ʿAzat-Emet*; iv.19, *Ruah-Emet*, *i.e.*, "the Holy Spirit"; viii.2, "doing *Emet* and *Zedek* and *Mishpat*"; 1QH,xiii.19, "all your acts are Truth and Righteousness"; xiv.2, "Men of Truth". For "Truth" associated with "the Way of God" in the N.T., see Mt 22:16, Mk 12:14, Jn 14:6, 2 Pe 2:2; in connection with "the Spirit", see Jn 14:17, 15:26, 16:13, 2 Th 2:13, 1 Jo 4:65; in connection with "Righteousness", see Eph 5:9; "Knowledge", 1 Ro 2:20, 1 Ti 2:4, Heb 10:26; "Judgement", Ro 2.2; "lying", "Tongue" imagery, and "the Enemy", Ga 4:10, 1 Ti 2:7, Ja 3:14, 1 Jo 1:6, 2:4, 2:21, 3:18; with "children of Light", Eph 4:8; with "walking"—another common Qumran allusion—1 Thess 5:5; and with "Perfection" and "Light", Ja 1:18.

[19] See above for 1QS's definition of "the sons of Zadok" as the *Shomrei ha-Brit*; the use of the word "service" in this allusion in Habakkuk also echoes the allusions to doing just such "Temple service" in the Zadokite Statement. We shall see it parodied below where the teaching of the Lying Spouter is concerned and further parodied in the eschatological end of the *pesher*. The phrase, *Britcha yinzor* (Deut 33:9), "your Covenant will he keep", actually occurs in the Messianic proof-texts conserved in 4QTest, as does its synonym, *lishmor et col mizvotai* (Deut 5:26). *Nozrei ha-Brit*, therefore, is simply a variation of the *Shomrei ha-Brit* terminology and the ideological root of the usage "Nazoraean". Further linkage of this phrase with Nazirite oath procedures popular in James' Jerusalem Community (Acts 21:23), life-long Naziritism associated with the persons of John the Baptist, James, and his ideological double *Banus* (which additionally provide the clue as to how the terminologies "sons of the Rechabites" or "Rechabite" priests are to be understood in relation to Jerusalem Christianity), and the *nezer* or "Branch", popular symbolism at Qumran, appealed to the sectarian love of word-play. See also the stress on "Doers" in Ja 1:22f.

1QpHab,viii.1ff.'s exegesis of Hab 2:4 below.[20] CD,iv.4 also identifies "the sons of Zadok" with "the Elect of Israel, ... men called by name to stand at the End of Days" or "men called by name" who in the manner of the primordial *Rishonim* or "Pillar" *Zaddikim*, like Noah in Hebrew Ecclesiasticus, "provide salvation for the earth" (ii.11).[21] The idea, presented in the context of strong atonement imagery, of being "called by name" or "naming names" in CD,ii.11ff. and iv.4ff. further connects all these allusions to the activities of the first *Zaddik* Noah, who was also portrayed in Genesis as "making atonement for the land". These ideas are not a little refracted in the strong emphasis on "name" and "naming" in Acts 2ff.

Having dealt with these preliminary matters, as it were, the text proceeds to its most important exegesis, that of Hab 2:4: "the Righteous shall live by his faith". This famous passage, the exegesis of which is again generally ignored in Qumran scholarship and which in our view is the ultimate *raison d'être* of the entire *pesher*, is found subjected to parallel, if divergent, exegesis in Galatians, Romans, and Hebrews. In conjunction with Is 53:11 and Gn 15:6 it forms the tripartite exegetical founda-

---

[20] This *yazdiku-Zaddik* imagery is inverted when the text has cause to refer to "the Man of Scoffing"/"Lying" who "pours out the waters of Lying on Israel" and "makes them wander astray in a boundariless wasteland" in CD,i.15ff. Both the usages, *nephesh* and "walking in Perfection", are used here relative to the "*Zaddik*", the former being part of the vocabulary of Is 53:11 upon which all references to the justifying activities of the *Zaddik* are based.

[21] CD,iv.5ff. *N.b.*, the parallel use in iv.11 of "*Beit*-Yehudah", which will play so important a part in 1QpHab,viii.1ff.'s exegesis of Hab 2:4 below. Iv.9 applies the theme of atonement, applied to the inner priestly elite in the context of spiritualized Temple and sacrificial offering imagery in 1QS,viii.1ff., to the activities of "the sons of Zadok"/"Men of the Perfection of Holiness". In all documents we are in the familiar atmosphere of Matthew and Luke's "not one jot or tittle". The reference to "standing in the Last Days" relates to the same eschatological imagery we shall encounter in the exegesis of Hab 2:4 below and is based, at least partially as we have suggested, on "the standing up of the bones" passage in Ez 37:10 (including the probable sense of resurrection, which is, in fact, the background sense of the entire exegesis of Ez 44:15 in CD,iv; cf. also "standing" in Dn 12:13 and its exposition in Lam.R,ii.3.6 in precisely this vein).

CD,i.16 denotes these primordial "Righteous Ones" by the terminology "the *Rishonim*", and it is to them the "first Covenant" was addressed, paralleling the *Aharonim* of the present generation, to whom "the New Covenant" of "the Last Days" applied (these last presumably to go into the Kingdom *living*). The *Rishonim* are to be identified with the *Anshei-Hesed/Zaddikim* of Hebrew Ecclesiasticus and Wisdom, the list of whom in the first-named work culminates with the *Zaddik* Simeon. It is in legitimatization of his "Zadokite" priesthood that Hebrew Ecclesiasticus evokes the Noahic "Covenant of Peace" vouchsafed to all descendants of Phineas (actual or figurative) because of their "zeal". *N.b.*, the purposeful inversion and/or trivialization of "the First" vs. "the Last" vocabulary in the Gospels, which takes its cue from Paul's allusion to himself as "last" in 1 Co 15:8 ("the First" according to his scheme being the "Jewish" Apostles or the Jerusalem Church leadership; "the Last" are Paul and his new "Gentile Christian" converts).

tion of early Christianity as it has been made known to us, providing, as we have noted, incontrovertible *textual* proof (as opposed to archaeological or palaeographic) that the *Pesher* relates to the fifties and sixties of the Common Era when such exegesis (however unfamiliar the present context, circumstances, and implications might at first appear) was in vogue. In the absence of an earlier indication of a similar exegesis, particularly prior to Herod's 37 B.C.E. conquest of Jerusalem, or even that this style of exegesis (which was in the view of the Habakkuk *Pesher* the seemingly exclusive prerogative of the Righteous Teacher in his role as exegete of "the last times") was even practised to any extent earlier than the mid-first century C.E.; the burden of proof rests rather upon those who would deny the historical provenance for the Habakkuk *Pesher* as we are setting it forth; not *vice versa*.

We have already shown that parallel usages and exegesis were employed in relation to the position and person of James in early Church literature. We shall be able to show that exegesis specifically applying the "cedars of Lebanon" imagery to the fall of the Temple in both the Habakkuk and Is[a] *pesharim* was also in vogue in Jewish sources regarding the fall of the Temple in 70 C.E. In addition, the exegesis of Hab 2:4 in the Habakkuk *Pesher* provides another interesting example of the basic parallelism between Qumran and New Testament exegetical styles. Not only is a reference to *zaddik* in the underlying text exploited to develop an exegesis about the Teacher/Messiah, but its sense is deliberately reversed, *i.e.*, we have to do not with "the Righteous" in the community "living by faith" as one would expect, but rather with the salvation brought about by this faith in the Righteous Teacher or Messiah. Put in another way, the usage *zaddik* in the underlying text is related, not to the individual believer, but rather to the object of his belief, as it were, the *Moreh ha-Zedek* or the Messiah. Actually the exposition turning on *zaddik* in the underlying text is double-pronged in both Pauline and Qumran exegesis, signifying at one and the same time both the Righteous Teacher/Jesus and those "saved" by their faith in him—at Qumran our "sons of Zadok"/"Elect of the last times" and in Christianity (though in no way as neatly delineated) "the children of the Promise"/"Community of all the faithful".

In the Qumran exposition of this passage (viii.1ff.), continuing the theme of the restriction of the provenance of the "delay of the *Parousia*" materials to "the Doers of the Law" that precedes it, the applicability of "the Righteous shall live by his faith" is, as it were, deliberately restricted not once, but in a two-fold manner. First, as above, to all "Law-Doers" (*'Osei ha-Torah*); and secondly, as if conscious of and completely opposed to the more permissive and cosmopolitan Pauline exposition of the same passage, *only to Jews*. What is left unstated, but nevertheless implied, is the negation of its contrary, *i.e.*, it *does not* even apply to anyone who *does not observe the Law outside the House of Judah*. It is surprising that it has rarely, if ever, been observed that the reference to "the House of Judah" in this passage (and elsewhere) quite simply refers to *Jews* and that the efficacy of this crucial theological proposition is here being restricted only to *Jews who are Doers of the Law*. Nothing could be closer to what we can assume to have been "the Jerusalem Church" exposition of this passage, opposed as it was according to all extant testimony, to the extensions via the Gentile Mission's new "free gift of faith" ideas to "Sinners", *i.e.*, all those born *outside the Law* or "born in sin".[22] Here the exegesis is not only "Jamesian", but framed seemingly with the express challenge of "the Gentile Mission"/"the Man of Lying" (who "spoke derogatorily about the Law in the midst of the whole congregation") in mind.[23] In regard to this last, we have already called attention to, in addition to New Testament narratives of problems between Paul and James, the Pseudoclementine account of an actual physical assault by Paul on James, which has via the magic of art probably received its literary transformation into an assault by *the Jews* (inclusive of Paul) on the archetypical *Gentile* believer "Stephen".[24]

---

[22] The allusion *Beit*-Yehudah in all probability goes back to the Jer 31:30f. passage on "the New Covenant". In this context in the Habakkuk *Pesher* it simply means "all Jewry", *i.e.*, the efficacy of the process of "salvation by faith" is deliberately being circumscribed to Jews alone. Gentiles, who had not first associated themselves with "the House of Judah" in the normal manner, are automatically excluded from its provenance. N.T. allusions to Jesus preferring the company of "Sinners" (linking up to the allusion *Resha'im* at Qumran, not to mention "prostitutes", "tax collectors", "gluttons", and "winebibbers") have important ramifications within this context. "Gentiles", who had not been born under the Law and were not therefore, to use Paul's own phraseology, heirs to its "promise", were automatically regarded as "Sinners" or "born in sin". Paul himself unequivocally makes the linkage between the "Sinner" terminology and "Gentiles" in Ga 2:15ff. For Jesus preferring the company of "publicans and Sinners", as opposed to "the Righteous" ("publicans" has interesting ramifications for 1QpHab,ix's "tax-farming" charges below), see Mt 9:10ff., 11:19, Mk 2:15ff., Lk 5:30, 6:32ff., 7:34, 13:2ff., etc. Note that Jn 9:31 knows very well that according to strict Jewish theory "God does not hear (the prayers of) Sinners", meaning in this context Gentiles. For an excellent example of such New Testament inversion, see Mt 21:33's contention that "the tax-collectors and prostitutes believed on" John. But the *historical John* incontrovertibly lost his life confronting precisely such persons, *i.e.*, tax-collectors and harlots.

[23] Cf. above 1QpHab,v.3ff. and the parallel allusion in CD,i.18ff.

[24] Rec 1.70. We have already pointed out in passing Paul's perhaps inadvertent application of such a vocabulary to himself in Ga 4:16. Cf. the parallel usages in Ja 4:4 and Mt 13:25's parable of the tares, where "the Enemy" (who can be none other than Paul) sows the evil tares and is finally identified as "the Devil". Paul over and over again shows his concern over the "Lying" accusation; cf. Ro 3:7, 9:1, 2 Co 11:31, Ga 1:20, 1 Ti 2:7, etc. 1 Jo 1:6, 1:10, 2:4, 2:21ff., 4:20, and 5:10 show the terminology was known to other authors in the N.T. 1 Jn 2:4 even places in conjunction the "Liar"-type with the activity

The Habakkuk *Pesher* puts the total proposition in the following manner: "God *will save* those Jews who are *Law-Doers* (if equivalent to "Covenant-Keepers", "Law-Doers" and "sons of Zadok" are synonymous) from *the House of Judgement* because of *their works and their faith* in the Righteous Teacher" (italics mine). Here there can be little doubt that we are in the typically "Jamesian" milieu of works/Righteousness, and where these and the issue of "faith" are concerned, as in the case of "Jews who were Law-Doers", the *pesher* would appear to have been framed with the express position of "the Enemy" in mind, *i.e.*, a man is not saved by his "faith" alone, but by "works" working with "faith" ("faith" in the effective stewardship of the Righteous Teacher). What often goes unremarked is that the explicit reference to "*ʿamalam*", apart from what we shall presently be able to identify as its eschatological thrust, places us (as later in x.12) squarely in the milieu and vocabulary of Is 53:11f.[25] It should not simply be translated "suffering", but rather "suffering works", or perhaps even more to the point, "works with soteriological effect". It closely approximates what is translated as "works" in the Letter of James, and we shall encounter it and its companion usages from Is 53 like *Daʿat* (Knowledge) and *Rabbim* ("the

---

of "not keeping his commandments". Ja 3:14f., including an allusion to "Truth", provides the evidence that this kind of terminology was applied to at least one of its ideological opponents. Cf. too Ja 1-2 on "Doers", "Breakers", etc.

[25] The *yazdik-zaddik* usage is to be found uniquely in Is 53:10ff. in connection with key Qumran terminologies like *Daʿat, nephesh, ʿamal*, and *Rabbim* (the usage in Is 5:23f. is slightly different, but it too finds an echo in CD,i.19). It is not often remarked that Qumran organization of *Moreh ha-Zedek* and *Rabbim* is itself reflective of Is 53:11's "justification" ideology, because the basic identity of the *Moreh ha-Zedek/Zaddik*, like the esoteric thrust of the usage "Zadok" related to it, is rarely grasped. The use of *ʿamal* in connection with "faith" in 1QpHab,viii.2, *i.e.*, that "the Righteous" are saved *both* by their faith and their works, ties up the exegesis of Hab 2:4 with that of Is 53:11 paralleling their same close "tie-up" in "Gentile Christianity". Paul, too, reveals that he was taught such an exegesis of Is 53:11, probably in Jerusalem by the *Jewish* apostles, in his 1 Co 15:3ff. introduction to his version of resurrection sightings: "I taught you *what I had been taught myself*, namely that Christ died for our sins *in accordance with Scripture*" (italics mine; that Scripture is almost certainly Is 53:12. The interpolation in the order of resurrection appearances which follows, can hardly be the phrase, "to James and then to all the apostles", as it is normally taken to be; but rather the patently inaccurate, "first to Cephas and secondly to the Twelve"—there were only eleven at the time and these must be understood as including "Cephas").

There are numerous references to "justification" at Qumran, expressed primarily through the *yazdik-zaddik* terminology, but also through the passive *yizadek*, *i.e.*, "to be justified". In this framework, it should be appreciated, *zedakah* differs somewhat from *Zedek* in that it carries with it something of the sense of the verbal noun "justification". In addition to *yazdiku* in conjunction with allusion to "Noahic" redeemers in CD,i.19 and the exegesis of "sons of Zadok" in iv.7, see 1QM,xi.14 (the eschatological "clouds of Heaven" section again) and 1QH,ix.9. For passive usage, see 1QS,iii.2f., 1QH,vii.28, ix.14f., xiii.16f., xvi.11, etc.

Many''),[26] as well as allusions to its analogue *ma'aseihem* and its variations, whenever the justifying activities of the Righteous Teacher or their ideological inversion are concerned in Hymns, the Zadokite Document, 1QpHab, 4QpNah, etc.[27] One should also note the reiteration of this same "Doers" phraseology in the first two chapters of the Letter of James, accompanied as at Qumran by its ideological opposite breaking/Law-Breakers.

When these aspects of the exegesis are properly recognized and taken in their eschatological sense, then the usage *Beit ha-Mishpat*, which Vermes and other commentators translate quite prosaically as "House of Judgement", and the consonant Hebrew *yazzilem*, "He saves them", take on a completely different sense. One does not have here an actual courtroom experience (except figuratively), but an allusion to "salvation" and the believing and commissionary activities required of those waiting for the "Day of Judgement".[28] This error is fundamental and it has clouded research on the Habakkuk *Pesher* more perhaps than any other. It is certainly remarkable that commentators persist in missing the eschatological sense of references to *"Beit ha-Mishpat"*, *"Yom ha-Mishpat"*, *"'amalam"*, and *"yazzilem"*/*"yazzilum"* in this *pesher*, just as they persist in missing the eschatological sense of CD,iv.2ff.'s exegesis of the Zadokite Covenant. When this exegesis is viewed in relation to the Pauline exegesis of the same passage, Ja 2:17ff.'s "faith without works" admonishment of "the Empty Man"/"Enemy" (which cites *the act* of sacrificing Isaac from the life of Abraham to counter the Pauline ideological position on Gn 15:6), the references at the end of this *pesher* in

---

[26] *Da'at* is used at Qumran as a fundamental conception. Again, it is rooted in the conceptuality of Is 53:11f., *i.e.*, that not only does the *Zaddik/Moreh ha-Zedek/Mascil* carry out his justifying activities through "suffering works", but also through "imparting Knowledge", *i.e.*, "teaching". As the Pauline "free gift of faith"/"grace" doctrines supplanted the original sense of these ideas, the teaching aspects of the Messiah/*Zaddik*'s activities were subordinated to the soteriological ones; but even in the highly refracted portraits in the N.T., traces of these former still persist. As time went on and the delay of the *Parousia* grew ever more certain, these allusions to "Knowledge" were easily transformed into the more powerful notation *Gnosis*.

[27] We have already noted the existence of the doctrine of "works", *i.e.*, *ma'asim* and its variations, at Qumran. In this passage and that on "the delay of the *Parousia*" preceding it, the connection of "works" to "works of the Law" is plain (not the variation of it one encounters in the N.T.'s "many marvelous works", which entails rather curing, exorcisms, raisings, and the like). The exegesis of "the Righteous shall live by his faith" is restricted to "Doers of the Law in the House of Judah" *only*. Certainly its eschatological thrust was never conceived of as applying to *non-Doers* outside this house.

[28] 1QpHab,viii.2; cf. 1QpHab,xii.14, where against a background of allusion to *Ebionim* ("the Poor"), "lying", etc., the same verb, *yazzilum* ("will be saved"), is used, this time in conjunction with the actual expression, *Yom ha-Mishpat* ("Day of Judgement"); the latter recurs in xiii.1ff. In xii.17, Ja 5:3's "gold and silver" is evoked in the context of the same kind of coming "Judgement".

x.3ff. and xi-xii to *Beit ha-Mishpat/Yom ha-Mishpat* (delivered in a milieu of contemptuous reference to "the Spouter's leading Many astray"/"instructing them in lies so that their *'amal* would be empty"), and condemnation of all Gentiles and idolators (including backsliding Jews); then it will be recognized that the exegesis does not refer to some trivial temporal dispute between Seleucids and Maccabeans, or some similar matter, but rather the developing *eschatological and theological framework* of early Christianity. When these matters are properly understood, then it will also be understood that the addition of *'amal* to *amanatam* ("their belief") in viii.2 was neither accidental nor incidental, but *a direct rebuke* to the Lying Spouter regarding his position on the same subject of the genre of that to the lying "Tongue" in Ja 3:5ff.

Having thus vented its spleen over overriding internal concerns (for which the modern commentator must be grateful), the text now shifts its attention to the second of its two antagonists—this one outside of the actual community itself and seemingly *directly* responsible for the death of the Righteous Teacher. The *pesher* is in its *denouement* stage and moving towards a conclusion. Along with it, the life of the Righteous Teacher is also moving into its final stages, not to mention (in the exegete's view) the history of the people as a whole. The background context, which is ongoing, is still the coming of the Romans and the ultimate destruction of the Jerusalem priesthood. This, it should again be emphasized, is still an event in progress and not necessarily complete. The exegete allows that the Wicked Priest "once enjoyed a reputation for Truth". Since he is very likely Ananus (or, as the two cannot always be safely differentiated, Ananias), one should refer to Josephus' comments about the former in the *Jewish War*. These comments are themselves remarkable, for they accord precisely with what Origen and Eusebius claim was written in the copies of Josephus available to them about Ananus' adversary and opposite number James.

Later Josephus reveals his true feelings about Ananus in the *Vita*, and these are hardly very flattering. In the process, he also testifies to the fact that Ananus ruled in the manner of an independent ruler.[29] Whether or

---

[29] 1QpHab,viii.8ff. Cf. above our comments about contrasting Josephus' portrayal of Ananus in *War* 4.5.2 with his comments in *Vita* 38 and *Ant.* 20.9.1. His account in *War* reads as follows: "He was on all accounts a venerable and very just man (*i.e.*, a *Zaddik*)..., who treated even the most humble people (*i.e.* "the Poor" or Qumran's *'Anayyim* or *Dallim*) with equality. He was a prodigious lover of liberty and admirer of democracy in Government and did ever prefer the public welfare before his own benefit..." These are startling words when one considers the parallel virtues accorded James in early Church testimony. In *Vita*, however, Josephus describes Ananus as "being corrupted by bribes" (with Josephus and John of Gischala he was involved in some sort of olive oil racket in the early days of the War in Galilee). In the *Ant.*, where he is most

not he did is not really germane, since the notice in the *Pesher* mentioning such rule (viii.9f.) need not relate to his actually "having ruled" in the secular sense, but simply to his having occupied the high priesthood. As we have seen, it is precisely this kind of reference (*i.e.*, "when he ruled Israel, his heart grew arrogant and he abandoned God and *betrayed* the Law", leading directly into the material about "stealing Riches"/"partaking of the Riches of the Gentiles" and the death of the Wicked Priest) which has always been used by scholars to press the provenance of the entire exegesis back into the Maccabean period despite the relevance of almost every allusion in it to events between the 50's and 60's C.E. Where the Maccabees, for instance, are concerned, there is absolutely no indication from any source whatsoever that rapaciousness was seen as one of their particularly noteworthy sins, which is *not the case* where the Herodian priesthood is concerned.

This theme of "stealing Riches" and "gathering"/"taking the Riches of the Gentiles"/"Violent Ones" is extended in ix.4ff. into a condemnation of "the last priests of Jerusalem" who "collected Riches and profiteered from the spoil of the peoples" (attached to a reference to "Gentiles" in the underlying text) generally. The translation of *"bezaᶜ"*, "profiteered from" or "were greedy about", is very important and sets the tone for appreciating the whole. Josephus tells us how Ananias, and by implication probably Ananus too, piled up Riches for himself by rob-

---

critical of his "breach of the laws" in dealing with James (*i.e.*, again the "Law-breaking" theme), he describes Ananus as "a bold man in his temper and very insolent".

Having just described in *War* how the common people "went with *the greatest zeal*" (against the high priests) and how the "Idumaeans" stood on Ananus' "corpse" and upbraided it because of "his kindness to the people", Josephus nevertheless intones: "I should think it not mistaken to say that the death of Ananus was *the beginning of the destruction of the city and that from that very day may be dated the overthrow of her wall and the ruin of her affairs whereon they saw their high priest and procurer of their preservation slain in the midst of the city*" (italics mine). The resemblance of this testimony to what Origen and Eusebius claim they saw in their copies of Josephus in relation to James' demise is uncanny. Even allusions like "a very just man" and "procurer of their preservation" reflect titles applied to James in extant literature like *Zaddik* and *Oblias* ("Protection of the People"). Josephus concludes: "I cannot but imagine that Virtue groaned at these men's case ("who had but little before worn the sacred garments and ... were cast out naked and seen to be the food of dogs and wild beasts"), and lamented that she was here so terribly conquered by Wickedness"; cf. the opposite sense given the same genre of "Wicked" vs. "the Righteous" scriptural passages applied in 1QpHab,i.11f. to the death of the Righteous Teacher and in early Church history to the death of James, as well as the whole presentation of "the Wicked Priest" destroying the Righteous Teacher, "the Men of his Council" (*i.e.*, "Lebanon"), and "the Poor" in ix.9ff. and xi.4ff.

All of these bizarre turn-arounds can hardly be coincidental and bear heavily on our identification below, pp. 49ff. of these passages in the Habakkuk *Pesher* as relating to Ananus. Josephus himself has, in fact, already shown us the way towards their resolution by the two opposing kinds of things he was willing to say about Ananus; we must assume that he was willing to say the same kinds of opposing things about James.

bing the tithes of the poor priests. He also specifically comments on the enormousness of his wealth.[30] That the various Herodian high priestly clans like "the sons of Ananus" behaved in just such a manner, including "using violence with the people", is also attested to in the Talmud in its preservation (despite the Phariseeism of its orientation) of what are referred to as "the Zealot woes".[31] This tension between "Rich" and "Poor" is reflected in Josephus' description in *War* 2.17.6 of how, after stopping sacrifice on behalf of foreigners, "the Innovators" encouraged "the Poor" to rise against "the Rich" and how as a consequence the palaces of Agrippa II, Bernice, and Ananias were burned, as were *the debt records*.

It is also reflected in the sudden appearance of the "Poor" appellations in this period, not only at Qumran, but on into Jewish Christian or "Ebionite" tradition and in Paul's descriptions of his relations with "the Jerusalem Community". These "Poor" terminologies are a concomitant to the second of the two "all Righteousness" commandments, *i.e.*, "Righteousness towards one's fellow man", which Ja 2:8f. calls "the Supreme Law of Scripture" (it is also cited in the Zadokite Document). Nothing could more accord with the condemnation of "the Rich"/"Riches" in James (sometimes echoed in the Gospels), Josephus' descriptions of "Essenes", and CD,iv's condemnation, *inter alia*, of the "Riches" of the Jerusalem establishment. The usage, which is developed in the last chapters of the Habakkuk *Pesher* in the context of the destruction which the Wicked Priest visited upon the Righteous Teacher and the members of his community (*n.b.* this "Poor" terminology is inclusive of the community leadership in contradistinction to "the Simple of Judah" notation which seems only to have applied to the rank and file), is with its two analogues *'Ani/'Aniyyim* (also *'Anavim* at Qumran) and *Dal/Dallim*, very widespread at Qumran. In general, all are used synonymously with some of the sect's other manifold forms of self-designation, *i.e.*, "sons of Zadok", "sons of Truth", "sons of Light", "sons of Righteousness", "sons of Piety", "men of the lot of Melchizedek", "Poor Ones of

---

[30] Aside from profiteering charges against Ananus in *Vita*, Josephus specifically calls Ananias "a great hoarder of money" in *Ant.* 20.9.2 directly following his description of James' judicial murder, and here and in 20.8.8 he describes how the high priests "sent their servants to the threshing floors to seize the tithes... so that the poorer priests died for want". For "Riches" charges, etc. against Bernice, see *Ant.* 20.7.3 and above, p. 9.

[31] Cf. b. Pes 57a and Tos Men xiii.21.533. The passage in question knows "the Boethusians, the house of Ananus, Kantheras, Ishmael b. Phiabi", etc. and ends with the lament that "their sons are Treasurers, their sons-in-law are Temple Captains, and their servants smite the people with sticks"; *n.b.*, the stress on the usage "the people" and that the tradition is ascribed to one "Abba Joseph b. Hanin".

Piety'', ''Enthusiasts for Righteousness'', etc.[32] This struggle between ''the Rich'' and ''the Poor''—the *sitz-im-leben* of James, as well as the cessation of sacrifice in the Temple on behalf of foreigners—also punctuates the struggle between the temporizing, more accommodating high priesthood, compromised as it was by its various Herodian connections, and the ''zealous'' lower priesthood, in which James appears to have played a crucial role.[33]

Where the Wicked Priest, in particular, is concerned, the theme of ''abandoning God and treachery to the Law'' is developed in terms of ''stealing Riches and gathering (in the sense of ''harvesting'' or ''collecting''—perhaps even ''tax-farming'', which sets up interesting resonances with the portrait of ''tax-collectors'' in the New Testament) the Riches of the Unruly Men who had rebelled against God'' (viii.11ff.). This ''Priest'' is also described as ''rebelling against and *breaking* the Laws of God'' (viii.16f.). The occurrence of the root *P-R-R* here, *i.e.*, ''breaking'' in the sense of Ez 44:7's ''Covenant-breaking'', ties the allusion firmly into the context of the Zadokite Statement's prohibition against admitting aliens ''uncircumcized in either heart or body'' into

---

[32] While J. Teicher did call attention to the use of the *Ebionim* (''the Poor'') terminology, its occurence at Qumran is much underestimated. While the parallel usage *ʿAni* does not appear in Habakkuk until 3:14, the terminology is introduced into the crucial exegesis of xii.2ff. It occurs in similar contexts in 1QM,xi.9ff., xiii.13f, and in 1QH,v.23 in conjunction with the term *Hesed* and *nephesh* (paralleling *nephesh-Zaddik* in CD,i) in ii.32, iii.24, and v.18, etc. Often it is used interchangeably or in conjunction with *ʿAni*, which must be translated as per N.T. usage ''the Meek''; cf. CD,v.21 and xiv.13. *N.b.*, Mt 5:3's ''the Poor in Spirit'' (as opposed to the Lk 6:20's ''the Poor'') precisely retains the sense of Eusebius' contemptuous references to the *Ebionim* in *E.H.* 3.27.1ff., *i.e.* they were ''Poor'' because of the poverty of their Christological conceptions; cf. also Mt 11:5, Lk 4:18 and 7:22, and Paul in Ro 15:26 and Ga 2:10 paralleled by James in Ja 2:2ff.

[33] For James' role among the lower priesthood during this struggle, see S.G.F. Brandon, *Jesus and the Zealots*, New York, 1967, pp. 182ff. We have already seen this same tension between ''Rich'' and ''Poor'' reflected above in Josephus' description of how, after stopping sacrifice on behalf of Romans and other foreigners in the Temple, ''the Innovators'' encouraged ''the Poor'' to rise against ''the Rich'' and burn the palaces of Ananias, the Herodians, and destroy all the debt records (*War* 2.17.6). Where James' custom of wearing only ''linen'' reported in all early Church accounts is concerned, Josephus pointedly describes how the lower priesthood won this right following his notice about James' death; *Ant.* 20.9.6. Another curious parallel is to be found in the description of Josephus' own Essene/''Rechabite''-style teacher cryptically denoted as ''*Banus*'' presumably because of his peculiar bathing habits. In *Vita* 2, Josephus tells us *Banus* wore only clothes growing on trees, by which he obviously means ''linen''. *N.b.* James' bathing habits are also the subject of a good deal of attention in early Church sources (even though the overt sense of these sources appears to contradict this notice in *Vita* about *Banus*). However, this is easily explained by referring to Josephus' description of the Essenes in the *War*, where he specifically notes that these same ''Essenes'' preferred ''being unwashed''. He means by this, *not that they never bathed*, but that they did not *anoint* themselves with oil in the Roman style, a constraint pointed out by all sources with regard to James as well. Like the ''*Banus*'' in Josephus' description, James too condemned ''fornication'' and was a vegetarian.

the Temple and the previous allusion to the *ᶜArizim/Bogdim, et al.* in ii.6 as
"Covenant-Breakers". Even the "uncircumcized heart" allusion will be
specifically applied to the Wicked Priest in xi.13. The allusion
"*Toᶜevot*"—"Abominations", another key element in the charges in Ez
44:6ff., and not inconsequentially those of the Temple Scroll, will also be
immediately applied to the Wicked Priest making it absolutely clear that
this section of the Habakkuk *Pesher* about the Wicked Priest is operating
within the context of Ezekiel's "Zadokite" Statement. For it, the Wicked
Priest, like the guilty establishment in Ezekiel and in contradistinction to
the *true* "sons of Zadok" in the Zadokite Document, is here being disqualified from service on the Temple Mount on the basis of Ezekiel's
charge of "admitting aliens uncircumcized in heart and uncircumcized in
flesh into the Temple" or what elsewhere it will call "unclean pollution"
or "polluting the Temple". The "breaking" charge is also reflected in
the "Law-breaking" one in the Letter of James and its mirror reversal
that of "Law-breaking" *against James* in *Antiquities'* portrait of James'
judicial murder. In *War* 2.17.10ff.'s portrait of these events leading up to
Ananus' death, Josephus also characteristically reverses this "pollution
of the Temple" charge, levelling it instead repeatedly at "the
Innovators" or so-called "Zealots" *in the Temple.*

The reference to "Unruly Ones"/"*Anshei-(H)amas*" as "rebelling
against God" also must relate in some sense to the *pesher's* earlier allusion
to *ᶜArizim* or "Violent Ones", not only described in ii.6 as "Covenant-
Breakers", but also as being treacherously involved with the Man of Lying—for CD,viii.37f. "the Men of War...walked with" or "turned
aside to the Man of Lying". The Habakkuk exegete notes that "he (the
Wicked Priest) partook of the wealth of the peoples" thereby "heaping
upon himself further iniquitous guilt" (viii.11f.; the resonance of
"heaped upon"—*losif*—here and "gathering"—*yikboz*—is intentional).
One should see in this allusion two separate processes of rapine both in
some way involving Gentiles—therefore the direct and overt accusation
of "guilt"—one using violence to plunder the tithes of the lower
priesthood (probably via the instrument of "unruly Gentiles" like
"Saulus" in the *Antiquities* or the other "Saul" in Acts who has a com-
mission to do violence from the Jerusalem high priests—following the
practice of Qumran and the "Temple wall zealots" we include Herodians among "Gentiles"/"*ᶜamim*"); the second relating to accepting
non-Jewish sacrifices and gifts in the Temple. Both are seen as equally
"abominable" where his priesthood is concerned and as undermining his
"good name".

The Wicked Priest's particular personal sins are delineated in viii.12f.
as walking in "the Ways of Abominations" (*n.b.* Ezekiel's "*Toᶜevot*"

here linked to an inversion of the "Way" terminology) and "unclean pollution" (*niddat-tum'ah*; viii.12f.). They are meticulously set forth in xii.7ff., which makes it absolutely *clear* that the first relates to the violence he did "the Poor", including the "destruction" of the Righteous Teacher and his associates for which he will be repaid a full measure of vengeance (as it turns out somewhat ironically by some of these same "Violent Ones"); the second, to "polluting the Temple of God", a charge specifically levelled against him in xii.8f. and which as witnessed by *War* 2.17.10, 4.3.12ff., etc. (including the language of "Abominations", "the Poor", "Traitors", "admission of foreigners", etc.) was "in the air" in this period. In both 11QT,xlvi.10ff. and CD,v.2ff., this "pollution of the Temple" charge is joined to one of not observing proper "separation" procedures in the Temple. The latter explains this in terms of not properly "separating" from people who "sleep with women in their periods" and "marry their nieces" as a matter of course. As its critique proceeds, including allusions to "removing the bound", preaching "wind", following "the Way of the people" (*'am*) and "kings of the peoples" (*'amim*—in our view Herodians), reference is made to their "evil Riches" and "ways of fornication", including even incest (CD,viii.5ff.), not to mention the charge of consonant "pollution...of the Temple treasure" (vi.15f.; there was *only one group, and one group only*, in this period that could be thought of as "sleeping with women during their periods" and "marrying nieces" as a matter of course—Herodians; see Appendix for more details of these charges).

We have already put forth the view that these Violent Ones included an assortment of unruly Herodians and others, as for example Saulus "the kinsman of Agrippa" (the intermediary between the accommodating Jerusalem establishment "desirous for peace" and the Herodians) and those of more revolutionary sentiment like Silas, Niger, Queen Helen's son Monobazus (in *War* 6.6.4 even his family at the end deserts the revolution and returns to the Roman fold), etc. While the *pesher* seems to imply some of these were used by "the chief priests" in matters of predacity, tax-collecting, and violence, others turn against these very priests and, as so often occurs in such circumstances, devour their former masters. We have already connected the allusion "*'amim*" in viii.12 and ix.5 to the two problems of "profiteering" operations in which "violence" was used against "the Poor" and receiving gifts from Gentiles in the Temple (cf. the specific underlying reference to *Go'im* in ix.3); but "*'Arizei-Go' im*" (4QpPs 37,ii.19 and iv.10) like Niger and Silas are in turn also among the principals in the early phases of the violent stages of the uprising at the time of what apparently seemed to be the miraculous discomfiture of Cestius.

In the course of describing the destruction of the Wicked Priest, the text, as we have already seen, discusses the related fate of ''the last priests of Jerusalem'', who it contends ''gathered Riches and profiteered from the spoil of the peoples''. These ''profiteering from''/''partaking of'' the ''spoil''/''Riches of the peoples'' accusations may simply be part and parcel of the kind of war-profiteering/''corruption by bribes'' charges Josephus levels against Ananus in the *Vita* 38. However it is more likely they imply involvement with Herodians and other violent ''Gentiles'', *i.e.*, that ''the peoples'' are those gathering ''the spoil''/''Riches'', from which ''the priests'' are profiteering. For 1QpHab,ix.5f., ''their Riches together with their booty'', *i.e.*, of the ''*Cohanei-Yerushalaim ha-Aharonim*'' (''the Last Priests of Jerusalem''—*n.b.* the plural sense here consonant with characteristic Herodian catch phrases like ''chief priests''/''high priests'') would ''in the last days be given over to the hands of the army of the *Kittim*, for they are the remnant of the peoples'' (*yeter ha-ʿamim*; ix.4ff.) Here the term ''*yeter ha-ʿamim*'' in the underlying text is specifically applied to the *Kittim*/Romans in the *pesher*, and there is an additional intended irony where those who advocated a policy of accommodation with foreigners (inclusive of Herodians) are concerned. As these priests used Gentiles ''to rob the Poor'' (cf. CD,vi.16) and also enriched themselves by accepting illegal gifts/sacrifices from these or other Gentiles (here the use of the word ''*ʿamim*'' to represent Herodians is pivotal), so too would ''additional Gentiles'' not part of these original Gentiles devour the ill-gotten gains and ''booty'' they had thereby amassed for themselves.

It is virtually inconceivable that this vivid picture could relate to any conquest earlier than 70 C.E., in connection with which Josephus in *War* 6.8.3 specifically tells us how the Romans extracted the secret of the whereabouts of the Temple treasure from the last Treasurer Phineas. This is to say nothing about the portrait's eschatological note about ''the last times'' (cf. the parallel between ''last times''/''last priests'' and the usage ''the Last'' generally denoting the final generation) and the sense, rendered by the present and future tense of the verbs of events in progress, not completed. If it relates to any earlier conquest, it is difficult to understand which, as one cannot point to any similar allusions or parallels in any earlier period. Nor would anyone have thought of applying a plural like ''last priests'' to the Maccabees, for plural terminologies like the ''high priests'' or ''chief priests'' imply an alignment of principal families and cannot in any real way be thought in terms of the more monolithic Maccabean structure. Nor can there be any doubt, as we have seen, that the Herodian high priests at this time plundered the tithes of the poor priests and accepted Herodian and Roman gifts in the Temple.

The criticism that for the exegete to be discussing these events, they must already have happened is as far from the mark as thinking these "last priests" in "the end of days" could in any sense relate to the Maccabean establishment, or what is even more far-fetched, a prior one. As we have already noted, any realistic observer, even those on Masada, at Qumran, or in the mysterious "Pella" haven of the Jerusalem Community, would have been quite capable of realizing this end was inevitable. In fact, after 68 C.E. these "last priests" had virtually already been destroyed and it only remained for their wealth to be given over to the Romans—which was in the circumstances an inevitability. The atmosphere of the *pesher* is so immediate and so tragic that it is hard to escape the impression that it was being set down almost simultaneously with the events it depicts. Still, there is nothing either archaeologically or palaeographically which would make its composition after 68 C.E. an impossibility.

Having described the "iniquitous guilt" and "Law-breaking" of "the Priest" (meaning here "the high priest"), his "Abominations" and "unclean pollution" (of the Temple) engendered by his greed, his 'skimming' *Gentile* "spoils" and depradations on "the Poor", the text describes the fate that overtook him and the vengeance that was visited upon him. It asserts that the Wicked Priest was "stricken by the Judgements upon Sinning" (ix.1f.). Because this Wicked Priest destroyed "the Righteous Teacher and the men of his Council", or at least committed very grave iniquity against them "dealing so wickedly with His (God's) Elect" (again the synonym for "the sons of Zadok" through whom "God would *execute Judgement on the Gentiles* and those of His own people *who kept the Law only when convenient*"—italics mine); he would be "delivered into the hands of his enemies that they might scourge him and consume him with bitterness of soul" (ix.9ff.).

Whether or not this accurately portrays Ananus' end or for that matter that of any other known candidate for Wicked Priest cannot be said with certainty. What is clear, however, is that Ananus did deliver James and some of his followers over to be stoned;[34] and, as the Uprising moved into its final phase, was caught by the "Idumaean" supporters of "the Innovators", whoever might be intended by these circumlocutions. He was

---

[34] *Ant.* 20.9.1. *N.b.*, the notice in CD,i.16ff. about the attack on the *Righteous One* also includes reference to an attack on several of his followers, but this probably rather relates to an earlier attack on James recorded in the Pseudoclementines, in which he was left for dead, but only broke his leg when he fell from the Temple balustrade. Josephus' charge in the *Antiquities* against James of "Law-breaking" can only have a basis in fact in the context of the *Yom Kippur* atonement on behalf of "the people" (*i.e.*, the ʿ*am*; according to our understanding, a "Zadokite" atonement understood according to the esoteric sense of the term) described in all early Church accounts of his death.

tortured and "horrible ignominities" (what in modern terms might be
called "atrocities") were inflicted upon his flesh. His enemies, in the
pesher's own words, did in a very real sense "take vengeance upon his
lifeless *corpse*", and Josephus specifically informs us that "the
Idumaeans" stood over his corpse and "abused" it with jests before
declining to bury it and throwing it outside the walls as food for the
jackals. Though the phraseology of this key allusion in the *pesher* is usually translated somewhat obscurely in a manner similar to Vermes' "they
took vengeance upon his body of flesh", the actual translation must run:
"they took vengeance upon *the flesh of his corpse*" (italics mine). The word
"*geviot*" here is also pivotal and certainly in this context has the sense of
"lifeless corpse", not "living body". It, along with "*abeit-galuto*" below,
relates the events in this *pesher directly* to Ananus' fate in a way that cannot
be claimed for any other candidate for Wicked Priest. As per Josephus'
presentation of the death of Ananus in the *War* (in contradistinction to
that which the early Church fathers report concerning the death of
James), the description here of the destruction of the Wicked Priest is *immediately* followed by those materials we have outlined above relating to
the destruction of Jerusalem and the Jerusalem priestly establishment.
This sequencing and the allusion to "corpse"/"*geviot*", in our view
"prove", as much as anything can, the relevance of these materials to the
extant data and historical context to which we have been linking them.

The usage "Judgements on Sinning" is also important here and links
up with the earlier discussion of Hab 2:4 and the climactic finale of
"Judgements" which the *pesher* will go on to delineate. Its plural sense
parallels the plural sense of and denunciation implied by "the horrors of
ignominious pollutions" or "diseases" attached to the description of the
violation of "the Priest"'s corpse, and both carry with them the very
definite implication of "vengeance", *i.e.*, in our view, vengeance for the
death of James (ix.1ff.). The latter, in particular, is obscure and need not
specifically relate to a person actually having suffered a disgusting
physical disease as it is usually taken to mean (though Ananus like
anyone else might have been suffering from some disease), a doubtful
proposition since such a disease would have disqualified him or any other
proposed Wicked Priest from the office of the high priesthood and
nothing is said in any of our sources about such a disqualification. Since
it parallels the reference to these divine "Judgements" (the plural sense
of which recurs in a more eschatological context in x.12), it is difficult to
escape the conclusion that it relates to the disgusting treatment meted out
to his corpse and a consonant divine disapprobation attached to this. Any
other reading is, in fact, impossible here, since the plural verbs "inflicted"/"committed" confirm these as *acts done to him*, *not* diseases. The

whole properly reads: "*They inflicted* the Judgements on Evil *by committing upon him* the outrages of evil pollutions *in* taking vengeance upon the flesh of his corpse" (italics mine). In his description of these events in *War* 4.5.2, Josephus makes mention of just such "impiety", and treatment of this kind, as in the case of crucifixion or beheading, was meant to cast the victim into a sort of divine disapprobation and the public disrepute consonant upon it. While Josephus, good Pharisee that he is, is horrified by the treatment accorded Ananus' corpse, it should be noted that the unknown author of the Habakkuk *Pesher* views the violation of the body of the Wicked Priest with equanimity.[35]

---

[35] Cf. Josephus' comments on the beheading of Antigonus in *Ant.* 15.1.2. Such "defilements" were probably also thought to constitute an impediment to resurrection. In *War* 4.5.2 Josephus does not conceal his own repugnance, and it is not without interest that he first makes mention here of the care Jews usually showed in the burial of the dead, that even "those condemned and crucified were taken down and buried before the going down of the sun", a notice not lost on Gospel tradition. The phrase, "he rebelled against and betrayed the Laws of God" (viii.17f.), has meaning within Josephus' specific acknowledgement that the "more fair-minded" among the populace thought Ananus had done precisely this in his illegal treatment of James. In addition, as we have seen, this phrase and description would most certainly have been applied by the sectaries to the ongoing confrontation in the Temple over the issue of sacrifices by foreigners, etc., labeled "pollution of the Temple" here and later in this *pesher*, as well as in CD,iv.18ff.

Where the execution of James is concerned, it should be noted, there is a very definite causality in the events leading up to his death and from it, to the fall of the Temple (as per early Church versions of Josephus). First, Josephus' so-called "*sicarii*" murder the former high priest Jonathan, brother of the Ananus presently under consideration and brother-in-law to Caiaphas (*Ant.* 20.8.5). There follows the "Temple wall" affair centering around the attempt by the Temple "zealots" to block Agrippa II's view of the sacrifice while he was lounging, presumably in the Greek manner, at dinner (*Ant.* 20.8.11; if Agrippa was not keeping Jewish dietary law, but rather eating in James' words "food sacrificed to idols", the insult would be all the more grievous). This triggers a Paul-style appeal to Nero on the part of "the Innovators". Almost immediately thereafter Agrippa II and Ananus take advantage of an interregnum in Roman governors to accomplish the judicial murder of James (*Ant.* 20.9.1). Shortly thereafter, Josephus undertakes his puzzling mission to the Empress Poppea to obtain the release of certain "Essene"-type priests still imprisoned in Rome. There follows the fire in Rome blamed by Nero on what are considered to be "Christians", after which the repression in Judea mounts to a fever pitch, finally provoking the Revolt that is proclaimed by the lower priest class who halt sacrifice on behalf of Romans and other foreigners. It is this last, it should be noted, which Josephus condemns as "an innovation", even though it was not, and which, he informs us elsewhere, in a moment of presumable inadvertence, was inspired by the Messianic "Star" prophecy.

One is entitled to ask, what was behind this series of events? Certainly the same agitation is behind the visit of Simon to Caesarea in 44 C.E. to inspect Agrippa I's household arrangements that is behind the "Temple wall" affair, which ultimately leads to Agrippa II being barred from Jerusalem and the Temple altogether and the stopping of sacrifice in the manner demanded in Ez 44:7ff. on behalf of Romans and other foreigners. Our answer, provable or not, is that Agrippa II and Ananus certainly considered they were removing the symbolic center of this agitation when they removed the incarnate "Righteous One" (*Zaddik*), "Pillar", and popular leader of his generation, "James the Just".

The eschatological sense of "the last times" and "the last priests", and the whole emphasis on "Judgements" and vengeful destruction, is given further reinforcement in the next section (x.3ff.) about "the Judgement...of fire and brimstone" or "the Judgements of fire" which "God will make in the midst of the many nations". In the process, precise definition is given to the "*Beit ha-Mishpat*" terminology so crucial to the earlier exegesis of Hab 2:4. Vermes, who previously rendered it "House of Judgement" (and who rendered *geviot* above "body of flesh"), now renders it "the condemned House" ("whose judgement God will pronounce"), but the phrase is *eschatological*. It is discussing "the Judgement ... of fire and brimstone" which God will make "in the midst of many nations" (4ff.), and the theme of such a coming eschatological "Judgement" will dominate the *pesher* until its conclusion. It must be translated as "the Judgement that God will make when he comes to execute Judgement among the nations," and understood in terms of that "Judgement" which the *pesher* has already insisted will be the prerogative of and executed by "His Elect" (*i.e.*, "the sons of Zadok").

The underlying text now moves directly on to an allusion to "building a city with blood and erecting a town on Falsehood" (Hab 2:12f.), and the *pesher* exploits this and the eschatological note leading up to it to return to its favorite topic and seemingly overriding concern, its ideological battles with "the Man of"/"Spouter of Lying". In particular, the expression "Falsehood" in the underlying text is connected to its complaints about "the Pourer out of Lying", *i.e.*, the *Mattif ha-Cazav* (x.6ff.). The allusion to "Pourer" here (x.9, instead of the earlier "Man of Lying" in v.11), testifies to the basic interchangeability all of these terminologies. The additional implied parody it carries of baptismal procedures associated with this adversary (continued in x.14ff., though the text is defective, moving on into further eschatological reference to "the Day of Judgement" and "Judgements by fire") is made even more explicit in the Zadokite Document's parallel allusion (about an attack on the *Zaddik*; CD,i.10ff.). There, the *Ish ha-Lazon* ("the Man of Jesting"/"Scoffing"/"Comedian") "pours out (*hittif*) on Israel the waters of Lying" (*maimei-Chazav*) and "leads them astray in a wasteland without a Way" (*n.b.* the play on "Way" and "wilderness" allusions, the whole relating to "removing the boundary markers" of the Law). From 1QpHab,x.10ff. to xii.11, another of these interchangeable usages, "*Sheker*" ("Lying"), is introduced into the *pesher*, though it is not found in the underlying biblical text, and combined with reference to the *Mattif ha-Cazav* who "leads Many astray ... instructing them ("the Many") in *ma'asei-Sheker*" (*i.e.*, "works of Lying"). In 4QpNah,ii.7ff. these kinds of "lying" and "deceit" allusions are linked to "Tongue" imagery (as they are in 1QS,iii), which also forms the background of allusion to the brazenness of the ideological adversary in Ja 3:5ff. (as we shall see, the "Empty Man" allusion in 2:20 linking up with the "empty" *'amal* allusion in x.10 below). In 1QH,ii.31 and iv.9f. the expression *Malizei-Cazav* (best translated as "the Lying Deceivers") completes the circle of these various parallel allusions and demonstrates them to be basically variations on the same or similar themes.[36]

In its attempt to expound this allusion to "building a city with blood and erecting a town on Falsehood", the *pesher* provides an esoteric exposition of such surprising content that its meaning has eluded many commentators. When Paul's teaching "spiritual things spiritually" thesis is properly taken into account and when it is understood that the "building"/"foundation"/"erecting" imagery employed here parallels the kind of imagery he uses in 1 Co to develop his ideas on "Holy Communion", then it can be expounded. Beginning with a parody of the Righteous Teacher/*Zaddik*'s proper justification activity of "making Many Righteous", it contends, as we have seen, that "the Pourer out of Lying ... led Many astray in order to build a worthless city on blood and to raise a congregation on Lying". The addition of the allusion "worthless", the shift from "erect" in the underlying Biblical text to "raise", and from "town" to "congregation on Lying" (since *'Avlah* does not mean precisely "Lying") are all significant. We have already identified the "leading astray" imagery, used in CD,i.15 in conjunction with "the

---

[36] Often these kinds of allusions are viewed in conjunction with another expression *remiyyah* ("deceit"); cf. how this last expression is used in relation to the expulsion of backsliders from the sect and to the "Way in the wilderness" allusions of 1QS,vii.5f., viii.22, ix.8, x.23, etc., after already having been employed in the same document relative to baptismal allusions in iv.9 and 23. 4QpNah,ii.1ff. even understands the allusion "city of blood" in terms of "walking in Lying and Falsehood", which in turn is connected to an allusion to "those who Seek Smooth Things at the end of days". This "Lying" imagery together with "fornication", "Tongue", "lips of deceit", and "leading the Many astray" allusions is further developed with regard to a group called "Ephraim" or "the Simple Ones of Ephraim" in ii.7ff and iii.4ff. In these passages about "Ephraim"/"city of blood", as well as those about "leading Many astray"/"tiring out Many with worthless work", the hint of what were seen as illegitimate Pauline activities abroad by the Jerusalem Community (or the one at Qumran) should not be missed.

For our exposition of these puzzling usages, together with their link-up with "the Pharisees" and all "those seeking accommodation with foreigners at the end of days", see below, p. 55. The *sitz-im-leben* of these allusions is also clear and constitutes the retrospective historical perspective of the Nahum *Pesher*. Josephus provides it in *War* 2.17.1ff., when he links "all those desirous of peace" with "the Men of Power (*i.e.* the Herodians), the high priests, the principal of the Pharisees" and one "Saulus", who had already led a riot in Jerusalem and who was the actual go-between to Agrippa II, who was residing outside the city because he has been barred from it by "the Innovators". Not only did this alliance object to stopping sacrifice on behalf of Romans and other foreigners by "the Innovators", but Josephus describes it as *actually inviting* the Roman soldiers into the city to suppress the insurrection.

Liar"'s "boundary-removing" activities, as the ideological opposite of the "keeping the Covenant"/"Law" and "justifying" activities of the true "sons of Zadok". There, it also carried an implied parody of both Is 53:11's *yazdik-zaddik* ideology and Is 40:3's "Way in the wilderness" imagery. The parody of the former is consolidated in this particular passage by the pointed employment several times of the term "*Rabbim*", also used in Qumran organizational documents to describe communal membership.

This inversion of the "*Rabbim*" terminology is repeated in the very next sentence, this time in relation to "the Liar's tiring out Many with worthless work" (here expressed as *ᶜavodah* or "work" in the sense of "mission" or "service"; x.12). It is immediately followed by the employment of another key term from Is 53 justification theorizing, *ᶜamal*, already encountered in the exegesis of Hab 2:4 above. Both will be followed up in x.14 by the use of a third such usage from the vocabulary of Is 53:11, "*Daᶜat*" or "Knowledge", which, as we noted above, will be related to what appears to be an evocation of either Spirit or water baptism. Before, we identified "*ᶜamal*" as the distinguishing characteristic (along with "*Torah*-Doing") of the "Jamesian" or Jerusalem Church exposition of Hab 2:4, defined it as "works" (more precisely "suffering works"), and connected it with the Letter of James' insistence that "faith without works is dead". Here the *pesher* contends that "their works (*ᶜamalam*, *i.e.*, the "works" of the community that was built on "blood" and raised on "Lying", not "on the Law") would be empty", *i.e.*, "empty" of soteriological content and inefficacious. Not only should the implicit rebuke here to Pauline faith doctrines be obvious, but, in particular, there is the implied rebuke to Paul's exposition of Gn 15:6 that Abraham's "faith counted for him as Righteousness", *i.e.*, "faith without works" in this eschatological scheme "counted for nothing". In what must be seen as yet another strong verification of our presentation, Ja 2:20 at this point actually applies the word "empty", which the Habakkuk *Pesher* uses to describe the soteriological efficacy of those "works" emanating out of "the Liar"'s teaching, to the very person of its interlocutor, *i.e.*, "Empty Man" or "Man of Emptiness", implying thereby that just as the "faith" he taught was "dead", the "works" predicated upon it were "empty" or "of emptiness".

The addition of the word "worthless" (*shavo*) to the underlying "city on blood" phraseology, which we have already remarked above, like the subtle shifting of the underlying "Falsehood" to "Lying" in the exegesis, is also purposeful. This reference to "worthless" (*shavo*) is repeated in the next sentence, where "the Liar"'s "work (*ᶜavodah* as opposed to "works"—*maᶜasim*/*ᶜamal*) is characterized as "worthless".

"*Shavo*"/"*shaveh*" is also to be found in 1QH,ii.22, vi.4f., and vii.34 in the context of allusions to similar "laying the foundations" and "congregational" activities. It should be noted that where 4QpNah,ii.1ff. (in our view hostile to both Herodians and Pharisees) uses the imagery of "walking in lying and deceitfulness", it is also expounding the notation "city of blood". Not only does it do so (not coincidentally) in connection with an allusion to *overseas messengers*, it ties the notation to another puzzling notation—"Ephraim"/"city of Ephraim". 4QpNah,ii.9 goes on to expound the latter allusion in terms of "the Tongue of their Lies" and selling "fornication to the Gentiles", which it interprets in terms of "leading Ephraim astray"/"leading Many astray" (*n.b.* again the telltale vocabulary of 1QpHab here and the extremely pregnant allusions to "Lying lips" and "deceitful teaching"). If one interprets 4QpNah's "Seekers after Smooth Things at the end of days" in terms of "seeking accommodation with foreigners" (in the context of which both Pauline and Pharisaic cooperation with what was seen as the "fornication" of the Herodian family was pivotal), then the "Ephraim" allusion can be seen *inter alia* as inclusive of Pauline missionary activities overseas (cf. its use in just such a context and with just such effect when the hope is expressed in iii.5ff. that "the Simple Ones of Ephraim ... will forsake those who mislead them and *join themselves* to Israel"—italics mine).

In such an ideological framework, the usage "city" or "community" is not difficult to elucidate; nor is the constant recourse to "building" or "laying the foundations" in this *pesher*, 1QS, and Hymns. Mt. 5:14f. in the Sermon on the Mount makes oblique reference to the community as "city" both in the context of "Light" imagery and allusion to "works"; and in Ga 4:26 Paul (responding to the "enemy" charges) refers to "the Jerusalem above", interpreting it to include those "born in the Spirit" and "free", not those "zealous" slaves who "wished to be under the Law". Heb 12:12ff. even uses citizenship imagery to describe this "heavenly Jerusalem", calling everyone in it "a firstborn son and a citizen of Heaven".[37] Even more germane for our purposes, in 1 Co 3:9ff. Paul uses the kinds of "building" and "laying the foundations" imagery the *pesher* uses when he describes his community as "God's building" and refers to himself as "the architect." He finally concludes with a picture of his followers as "the Temple of God".

This latter must be seen as generically related to both the "heavenly Jerusalem" and "building" imageries. With regard to it and in the context of discussing James' directives on "fornication" and "food sacri-

---

[37] For more on Paul's view of adoptionist sonship, see his discussion of "the children of the promise" in Ro 9:7ff., which grows out of his discussion of spiritual sonship in Ro 8:14ff.

ficed to idols" and his own notion of "communion with the blood of
Christ" in 1 Co 10:16ff., Paul develops a portrait of the members of his
community as one body in contrast to "the other Israel" (*i.e.*,
1QpHab,viii.1's "House of Judah"). He continues this spiritualized
body imagery in 12:12ff., where he designates them, not only as the
Temple, but straightforwardly as "the body of Christ" (this of course
connects with the famous saying in the Gospels linking Jesus' body, after
the resurrection, with the Temple). Eph 2:16ff. elaborates on this "single
body" metaphor while at the same time denying there are any "aliens or
foreign visitors", an allusion patently directed against those problems
concerning foreigners in the Temple we have already analysed above.
This imagery, it should be appreciated, is all "spiritualized" in the manner recommended by Paul in 1 Co 2:13 and includes both
"spiritualized" body and "spiritualized" Temple imagery. Like
Hebrews, Ephesians calls its congregationalists "citizens like all the
Saints and part of God's household". Using Paul's "building" imagery,
it summarizes the position by describing them as "part of a building with
the apostles and prophets for its foundations and Christ Jesus himself, the
Cornerstone. As every structure is aligned on him, all grow into one holy
Temple in the Lord and you too in him are being built into a house where
God lives in the Spirit". Precisely the same genre of terminological
approach and imageries are being employed (but in an atmosphere
of "keeping the Law", not "breaking" it) in 1QS,viii.1ff. Here
"Cornerstone" and "laying the foundations" imagery are invoked
in conjunction with allusions to "the Council" as a spiritualized "Temple"/"Holy of Holies" and "a sin offering"/"sweet fragrance" of
Righteousness (cf. in particular the strong allusion here to "the Cornerstone not swaying on its Foundations" and even the ideas of "keeping
faith in the land" and "atoning for sin" by "suffering afflictions"). We
have already called attention to this imagery of the Community Council
as Temple and spiritualized sacrifice/atonement in connection with the
parallel "pollution of the Temple of God with idols" themes in 2 Co
6:16ff., CD,iv, and 11QT,xlvif. at the end of Chapter One above.

   The notion of communion built on some form of a "blood" compact
appears to have been put forth very early on by Paul and those following
his ideological "approach". In particular, one should note in this regard
1 Co 10:16, 11:25ff., and 15:50, as well as Ro 5:9, Eph 2:13, 1 Pe 1:2
and 1:19, 1 Jo 1:7 and 5:6ff., etc. That abstention from "blood" was
part and parcel of James' "Jerusalem Council" directives is made clear
in Acts 15:20ff. and 21:25. That from 1 Co 6:12 to 10:33, beginning with
the typically Pauline proclamation, "for me there are no forbidden
things", the terms of these directives are being discussed, including "for-

nication'', ''blood'', ''things sacrificed to idols'', etc., should also be clear. The discussion rises to a fever pitch in conjunction with the ''building'' imagery and the first reference to ''communion with the blood of Christ'' when Paul pronounces in 10:25: ''Do not hesitate to eat anything that is sold in butcher shops; there is no need to raise questions of conscience'' (for Paul, a euphemism for ''questions of the Law'').

The horror with which these ideas, in particular that of the mystery religion-oriented ''community built upon blood'', would have been greeted at Qumran can be measured by CD,v.5ff.'s ascription of the cutting off of the children of Israel in the wilderness to the consumption of ''blood''. The very idea that a community could be ''built'', even figuratively, on the consumption of ''blood'' would have been greeted in the circles represented by Qumran and the Jerusalem Church with just the kind of contemptuous condemnation we find in 1QpHab's characterization of the Lying Spouter as:

> leading Many astray in order to build a worthless city on blood and erecting a congregation on lying; and for self-glorification tiring out Many with worthless service (*'avodah*) and instructing them in Lying works (*ma'asei-Sheker*) so that their *'amal* would be empty (or ''count for nothing'') when they were brought to those (same) Judgements of fire concerning which they themselves had villified and hurled abuse at the Elect of God.

Where Paul's relationship with the Jerusalem Church is concerned, the notes about ''self-glorification'' and ''tiring out Many with a worthless service'' have particular import. We have already distinguished the word *'avodah* from ''works'' as expressed by *ma'asim* or *'amal*. *'Avodah*, which is also the subject of some speculation where the genre of lying nemesis in the Community Rule is concerned,[38] is rather to be associated with the kind of ''work'' or ''service'' Paul takes to ''boasting about'' and glorifying in 2 Co and can in some contexts even be translated as ''mission''. For the *pesher*, those persons instructed in this manner, or part of this ''building'', ''community'', or ''city'', also ''insulted and hurled abuse at the Elect of God'' (in our view James and the ''Jerusalem Church'' leadership, or precisely those ''Pillars'' so strikingly and enviously evoked in Ga 2:9).[39] These ''insults'' or ''abuse'' would, *inter*

---

[38] See above n. 36. and CD,viii.30 and 1QS,ix.8, where the postulant is urged not to cooperate with such an individual in ''work'' and ''finances'' and where reference is made in parallel context to ''the *Anshei-Remiyyah*'', their work being the opposite of *'avodat-Zedek* (''the service of Righteousness'') and *'avodat-Emet* (''the service of Truth''; cf. Paul in 2 Co 11:15 on ''the Servants of Righteousness''). *N.b.*, that in Ga 4:16 Paul's actual words are: ''So your Enemy have I become by speaking Truth to you.''

[39] The defamation of the Jerusalem leadership in the Pauline corpus proceeds in almost a drum-beat fashion. It is most evident in Ga 2:5ff., 1 Co 9:2ff. (where Paul calls his communities his ''work in the Lord'' parallel to the meaning we gave to the Hebrew *'avodah*

alia, appear to involve calling down on the communal leadership precisely those curses, *i.e.*, that of the coming "Judgements of fire"/"Day of Judgement", that the *pesher* here and in its finale calls down upon them (and "Gentiles" and "idolators" generally). Viewed in its simplest

---

above), and 2 Co 11:2ff. and 12:12ff. In conjunction with these murmurings against and slanders of the leadership, he often anounces his view of the Law and salvation by faith, which is diametrically opposed to the Qumran position above and the Letter of James; cf. Ga 2:15ff.: "Though we were born Jews and not pagan sinners, we acknowledge that what makes a man Righteous is not obedience to the Law, but faith in Jesus... no one can be justified by keeping the Law"; Ga 2:21ff.: "If the Law can justify us, there is no point in the death of Christ... Are you foolish enough to end in outward observance what you began in the Spirit"; Ga 3:11ff. interpreting Hab 2:4 to mean "the Law will not justify anyone in the sight of God" and playing on this further in Ro 1:16f. by interpreting "Righteousness" to mean "God saving all who have faith—Jews first, but Greeks as well"; Ro 3:20ff. in almost a direct riposte to James: "No one can be justified in the sight of God by keeping the Law; all the Law does is to tell us what is sinful... a man is justified by faith and not by doing something the Law tells him to"; and summing up in Ro 9:30ff.: "From this it follows that the pagans who were not looking for Righteousness (how pregnant this saying now appears and how true) found it all the same, a Righteousness that comes of faith; while Israel looking for a Righteousness derived from the Law failed to do what that Law required... Brothers, I can swear to their (the Jews') zeal for God, but their zeal is misguided." (here, of course, is the ultimate play on Josephus' "Zealot" terminology and the true thrust of the combination of these terminologies becomes clear; for James in an opposite vein, see *inter alia* Acts 21:21).

Qumran makes its criticism of the type of position expressed here clear, as we have already seen, in the section preceding its description of the Community Council as "a Holy of Holies for Aaron... that precious Cornerstone whose foundations shall neither rock or sway in their place... a sweet fragrance": "Any man who enters the Council of Holiness to walk in the way of Perfection as commanded by God and who overtly or covertly (here the Hebrew is *remiyyah*, which Vermes mistranslates as "negligence", but the word is "deceit") transgresses one word of the Law of Moses on any point whatsoever shall be expelled from the Council of the Community and shall return no more; no man of Holiness shall associate with him further either in monetary affairs or in approach." This whole position is preceded by the directive: "Whoever has gone about slandering his companion shall be excluded from the pure meal of the congregation for one year and do penance (*i.e.*, "table fellowship"; cf. Paul's "Nazirite"-style penances in Acts 18:18 and 21:26)... Whoever has murmured against the community leadership shall be expelled and shall not return" (1QS,vii.15ff.).

Ja 2:9 puts the same position in the following manner: "If a man keeps the whole of the Law except for one small point at which he fails, he is still guilty of breaking it all", concluding in 2:21: "Do you realize you Empty Man that faith without works is useless." Its author shows his familiarity with the problem of lying: "But if at heart you have the bitterness of jealousy, or a self-seeking ambition, never make any claims for yourself or cover up the Truth with lies (cf. also "Doers" against a critique of "Tongue", "deceit", "fornication", and "Riches" in 1:2ff.). Principles of this kind are not the Wisdom that comes down from above; they are only earthly, animal and devilish" (3:14f.; cf. 1QS,iii.1ff.). He, also, demonstrates his familiarity with the "Enemy" terminology well known to Jewish Christian tradition and alluded to as well in the Gospels (Mt 13:25ff.): "Don't you realize that making the world your friend is making God your Enemy? Anyone who chooses the world for his friend turns himself into God's Enemy... Brothers, do not slander one another. Anyone who slanders a brother or condemns him is speaking against the Law and condemning the Law. But if you condemn the Law, you have stopped keeping it and become a judge over it" (4:5ff.; for Paul's "making the world" his friend, see 2

terms, the allusion, therefore, threatens those "instructed" in the Liar's "works" with that same *Mishpat/Beit ha-Mishpat* which the *pesher* earlier insisted would be executed via the hands of this "Elect of God" (CD,iv.3f.'s "sons of Zadok"). However it is viewed, these kinds of allusions, *at least where the Liar is concerned*, have little or nothing to do with the violent or "bloody" construction of an actual "city", but are almost always *completely* esoteric and ideological in nature.

For good measure, our commentator has added the condemnation on "instructing them in Lying works" (*ma'asei-Sheker*), which relates to that "Congregation on Lying" which the Liar is "raising" and is,

---

Co 9:19ff.: "I made myself a Jew to the Jews to win the Jews...To those who have no Law I was free of the Law myself...I made myself all things to all men...That is how I run intent on winning; that is how I fight, not beating the air").

In Ro 10:12 and elsewhere, Paul announces his desire to found a community that would "make no distinction between Jew and Greek". In our view this is precisely the kind of ambitions which characterize the Herodian family, particularly Agrippa I and his brother Herod of Chalcis, but also his son Agrippa II and very likely the latter's son "Aristobulus" (cf. Ro 16:11) in Northern Syria, Cilicia, and Lower Armenia. In Ro 13.1ff. Paul lays out his political philosophy, such as it is: "You must obey the governing authorities. Since all government comes from God, the civil authorities were appointed by God (here Paul attacks "the Zealots" on their own "philosophical" ground) and so anyone who resists authority is rebelling against God's decision...Good behaviour is not afraid of magistrates (the witnesses to the crucifixion of Jesus would have been interested in this point, as would the author of Ja 5:6ff.); only criminals have anything to fear...The State is there to serve God for your benefit...This is also the reason why you must pay taxes (Paul's view of the "tax" issue which so exercised the "Innovators" from 4 B.C.E. to 70 C.E.), since all government officials are God's officers. They serve God by collecting taxes" (this last point has particular relevance to the Gospel portrait of Jesus' "table-fellowship" with *tax-collectors*).

Doubtlessly my presentation of Paul's position on these matters will not be a popular one, but I believe the strong links between the Pauline approach and Herodian family ambitions are not difficult to appreciate. Paul's Roman citizenship is easily comprehended in such a context. Herodians had married into the Cilician royal house and, in addition, Paul hints at his own "Herodian" roots in Ro 16:11 above. The massive fear displayed at Qumran over the power of an individual of the "Pauline" genus and Paul's ready access into the circles of Jerusalem power as described in Acts also become comprehensible within such a framework. The reticence of the Letter of James and its meticulous avoidance of the same kind of slander that Paul permits himself in more unguarded moments, as well as James' seemingly endless indulgence of him, are also made comprehensible in such a context.

As we have seen, 4QpNah,ii.1ff. interprets "the city of blood" in terms of "walking in Lying" and "deceit", which in turn is connected to an allusion to "the Seekers after Smooth Things". If we see this as alluding at Qumran to all those seeking accommodation with the governing authorities, Roman or Herodian, which was true as much of "Gentile" Christians as it was of Pharisees and so-called "Herodians", then we put ourselves into a more realistic historical framework for grouping "the Man of Lying" in such a company. In any event, Paul, like Josephus, made no secret of his "Pharisaic" orientation. Both he and Josephus mean the same thing by this, *i.e.*, accommodating themselves to the powers-that-be and foreigners, and this orientation has retrospectively been assimilated into the portrait of Jesus in the Gospels, for all intents and purposes vitiating its historicity.

ideologically speaking, precisely the opposite kind of activity as that predicated of the Righteous Teacher. It is in connection with these "Lying works" that he invokes the *ʿamal* usage we have discussed above (and defined as "works with soteriological effect"). Had these "works" been full, not "empty", they might have saved them from these same "Judgements of fire"/"Last Judgement". Exploiting a transition in the underlying text where reference is made to "water...filling the earth with the Knowledge of the Glory of God" (Hab 2:14), the *pesher* now moves back to events relating to the Wicked Priest, the death of the Righteous Teacher, and the destruction of the Temple and/or Jerusalem, all easily paralleled in events relating to James the Just's life and surviving traditions connecting his death to the fall of Jerusalem. So incensed is Origen over this last, which he claims to have seen in the version of Josephus available to him, a claim supported by Eusebius, that he cannot resist castigating Josephus for not connecting the fall of Jerusalem to Jesus' death, not James'![40]

The *pesher*, while poorly preserved at this point, first relates these "waters" to the "Lying" activities presumably of "the Pourer"/"Spouter". However, seizing on the reference to "knowing the Glory of God" noted above, it goes on to delineate this "water" imagery in terms of an ideologically opposite "revelation" of saving "Knowledge". The *Daʿat* it invokes (also translatable as *Gnosis*) is a fundamental concept at Qumran. We have already signalled its relationship to the vocabulary and ideology of Is 53:11 when taken according to its *literal* sense, not to its superficial one, *i.e.* "through the *ʿamal* of his soul...and by his Knowledge (*Daʿat*) will my Servant the Righteous One justify Many." The *pesher* pictures this "Knowledge" as flowing over earth's creatures like "waters over the seas", imagery not unrelated to New Testament pictures of baptismal-like "descents of the Holy Spirit", language not completely alien to the vocabulary of Hymns and the Community Rule.[41] It should be seen, too, as related to a certain extent to "Mes-

---

[40] Origen's outrage is probably not a little connected with the notice's disappearance in *all* extant versions of Josephus; however, once again, we have historical elements relating to James' death assimilating themselves retrospectively into the narrative of Jesus' death; cf. Origen, *Contra Celsum* 1.47, 2.13, and *Comm. in Matt.* 10.17 and Eusebius, *loc. cit.*; also Josephus' parallel comments in the extant *War* 4.5.2 in n. 35 above. See, too, how in the total portayal of these events Josephus turns the "pollution of the Sanctuary" charge back upon "the Zealots"/"Innovators" finally blaming them for the destruction of the Temple and Jerusalem just as in our view the Habakkuk *Pesher* blames Ananus, the Liar, and such genre of individuals.

[41] 1QpHab,xi.1ff. CD,i.1 addresses itself to all those who "know Righteousness and understand the works of God" (cf. CD,ii.3ff.) and we encounter the same combination of "the Foundations of Knowledge and Wisdom" in 1QS,ii.3ff. The latter usages progress through baptismal imagery in iv.6ff. and iv.22 until the final passages in viii-x of such in-

sianic" water imagery, itself associated with rain-making, "the Son of Man coming on the clouds of Heaven",[42] "raining Judgement on all the evil ones", and the Noahic-style destruction that was going to overwhelm these last—though the relationship here is indirect, not intrinsic.

The text now returns to its final description of the destruction of the sect's leadership by its second nemesis the Wicked Priest and the coming ultimate eschatological *Judgement*. It refers to a mysterious angry or violent confrontation between him and the Righteous Teacher. This confrontation relates to or is presented in conjunction with problems surrounding *Yom Kippur* observances. Because of its language, it has never adequately been explained by any theory of Qumran origins. It would not be surprising if this confrontation was simply anonymous and not documented in the sources available to us. However, even here elements do link up, however tenuously, to traces of events conserved in our sources. As we have seen in our introduction, early Church sources are unanimous in testifying to James' atonement activities on the Temple Mount. Both Epiphanius and Jerome make it clear that these appear to have transpired in the course of a single day and in some manner involved James' entering the Holy of Holies. If accurate, they must be seen as relating to *Yom Kippur* devotions of some kind, sectarian or otherwise.

Continuing this catalogue of known information regarding James in this crucial period, Epiphanius also pictures James as *kneeling* to make an atonement of some kind (probably before *the Judgement Seat*) until "his knees became hard as camel's hide". Eusebius conserves the "kneeling" and "camel's hide" elements of this testimony, but prefers the more general reference to "Temple" or "Sanctuary". These astonishing

---

terest to us (in particular, viii.9, ix.17, x.9f., 13, and 25f.). Reference to "Knowledge" combined with baptismal and "Holy Spirit" allusions is omnipresent also in Hymns. For 1QpHab,xi.1ff. above, contrasting with "the waters of Lying" spouted by "the Deceiver" in the Zadokite Document, this "Knowledge" will be revealed to the right-guided members of the Elect of the last times "like waters of the sea in overflowing abundance", imagery which moves easily into the *Gnosis* of succeeding centuries.

[42] We have called attention to this imagery in 1QM,xi.7ff. and Ja 5 above. For the combination of the themes of Noahic destruction by flood and the Judgement coming on the clouds of Heaven, see Mt. 24:37 comparing the coming of the Son of Man to the days of Noah. This is further alluded to in 24:17, Mk 13:15, and Lk 17:27ff. and 21:21, ending with the allusion from Daniel of "the Son of Man coming in clouds with great powers and glory". Mt adds: "And he shall send forth his angels with a great sound of a trumpet and gather together his elect from the four winds..." The statement that "this generation shall not pass away till all these things be accomplished" has relevance, as we have seen, to the expression of the disappointment of such hopes in 1QpHab,vii.10ff.'s exposition of Hab 2:3. Mt 24:36's avowal that "Heaven and Earth shall pass away but my words shall not pass away", is developed with more precision in Mt 5:18 about "not one jot or tittle of the Law" passing away, and relates to Gos Th 11f., which itself is tied up with the pre-existent nature of the *Zaddik* of Pr 10:25—developed so straightforwardly in both Hymns and *Zohar*,i,53b's discussion of "Noah".

notices, despite their vividness, have been dismissed as pure fantasy, as we have seen. For his part, Josephus testifies that James was tried before a Pharisaic/Sadducean Sanhedrin on a charge of blasphemy, *i.e.*, pronouncing or causing others to pronounce the forbidden name of God. Together with some of his colleagues (the plural note is important for the presentation of events in the Habakkuk *Pesher*), he was stoned. In our view, this judicial murder was connived at by *both* Agrippa II and Ananus (a position, which will receive some support, even if oblique, in the *pesher*), and it is related to earlier confrontations in the Temple, confrontations also discernible through the highly refracted presentations of both the Pseudoclementines and Acts surrounding the matters we have been following in this study, most notably the Temple wall incident and attempts to bar both Agrippa I and Agrippa II from the Temple "as foreigners". In our view, James' entry into the Holy of Holies, however improbable it might at first appear, constituted a proper "Zadokite" atonement based on his "Noahic" nature, *i.e.*, a "Man *Zaddik Tamim*" or "Perfectly Righteous in his generation", and at least makes the "blasphemy" aspect of this charge more comprehensible.[43]

The *Pesher*, which turns on the reference to "wrath" and "feast days" in the underlying text, discusses how "the Wicked Priest pursued the Righteous Teacher to confound" or "destroy him with his angry wrath at the house of his retreat" (or "at the house where he was discovered"; xi.4ff.). The usage *"leval^{c}o"* (xi.5) does not appear in the underlying text, but it indicates strong action, and as it is used in a seemingly violent context, probably signifies "destroy", not "confuse". When linked to the esoteric understanding of Belial/Balaam as "consumer of the people" (developed in the Appendix), this signification is dramatic. It triggers the much vexed reference to *"abeit galuto"* which, while defective, is usually translated as "House of his Exile".

The latter notice, in particular, is obscure, probably the most obscure in the *pesher*. If, nevertheless, we attempt to fit it into the events we are discussing, it can be thought of with little difficulty as referring to a physical "exile" or "retreat" outside of Jerusalem as at Qumran.

---

[43] Cf. *Ant.* 20.9.1f. The narrative in Eusebius, Jerome, etc., *loc. cit.*, about James falling from the balustrade or pinnacle of the Temple, only to be stoned outside the walls, is a conflation of two separate attacks on James, one by "the Enemy" in the forties (perhaps related to the attempt by "Simon" to have Agrippa I barred from the Temple as a foreigner) and the other by Ananus (our "Wicked Priest") in the 60's, which did result in James' stoning. The first, as reported in Rec 1.70f., did involve a "fall" from the Temple stairs in which James broke either one or both his legs (such vivid details are not ignored with impunity; cf. the suspiciously similar "fall" "Judas Iscariot" takes in Acts 1:25f.). The detail about a "fuller" smashing James' skull would appear to relate to material in M. Sanh 9.6 concerning the similar punishment reserved for a priest serving at the altar "in a state of uncleanness".

However, since the evocation of it is followed by a parallel allusion to "a rest period" associated with *Yom Kippur* observances and since all of these events appear to transpire "in Jerusalem" (xii.7), it can with equal merit be thought of as simply referring to a *Yom Kippur* retirement of some kind, *i.e.*, that the Wicked Priest pursued him "in order to destroy (or consume) him with his furious wrath at the house where he retired" (to observe the fast) or "was concealed". Taken in this sense, it need not refer to a physical locale outside of Jerusalem at all. But when taken according to another of its root meanings, *i.e.*, "uncovering" or "discovering", it could with even more sense be read to refer to "the house where he was discovered". This, in fact, is how we would prefer to read it, *i.e.*, as relating in some manner to James' *arrest* (as we shall see below, if the *juridical* sense of the usage "*zamam*", which follows in xii.6, is taken into consideration and the various "his"/*o*'s attached to *beit-galut* carefully analysed, then the expression can be thought of as referring not only to James' arrest, but also to *his trial* which follows).

The note about "appearing to them during the period of their *Yom Kippur* observance to consume them and cause them to desecrate the fast day of their sabbath rest" (xi.7f.) relates to the plural "them"/"their" and may or may not involve the same events as the pursuit and attack on the Righteous Teacher preceding it above, though the use of "*leval⁶o*"/"*leval⁶am*" is common to both. The confusion surrounding these references to sabbaths, feasts, *Yom Kippur*, etc. has given rise to considerable discussion about calendrical differences between Qumran and Jerusalem. As in the instance of the "horrible contagions" allusion, since the notices are obscure, their meaning will probably never be completely known to us. Where "*abeit-galuto*", however, is concerned, two clear themes do emerge: that of some kind of confrontation probably involving the arrest and leading to the destruction of the teacher and some of his comrades and that of a desecration of the sect's *Yom Kippur* observances (whether different from those of the Wicked Priest or the same).

Strengthening our view of an arrest and consonant destruction (not simply verbal "confusion"), the theme of "destruction" is further developed in the conclusion of the *pesher* where "the Simple of Judah doing *Torah*"/"the Poor" are the subject (and where it is expressed quite straightforwardly as "*lechalah*"/"*lechalot*" and linked to the "*zamam*" we noted above, *i.e.*, "intrigue"—even *judicial intrigue*; xii.2ff.). However, even before this in xi.15, it can be readily ascertained from the manner in which "*teval⁶enu*" is turned around and applied to *the fate of the Wicked Priest* instead of that of the Righteous Teacher and his companions, that our initial description of "*leval⁶o*"/"*leval⁶am*" as connotative of "destruction", not "confusion"/verbal confrontation, was correct. The exegesis in xi.11ff. turns on the reference "to the cup of the Lord's right hand" in Hab 2:16. In this context, the *pesher* also accuses the Wicked Priest of "not circumcizing the foreskin of his heart" (xi.13). As we have seen above, this allusion from the context of "the Zadokite Covenant" in Ez 44:9 relates to the barring of *both* "those uncircumcized in heart and those uncircumcized in body" from the precincts of the Temple. When applied to a *Jewish high priest*, it not only has the force of disqualifying him from Temple service in specifically "Zadokite" terms, but is of the utmost import vis-a-vis the difficulties and confrontations between "Innovators" and Herodians in the Temple and elsewhere at the root of the problems we have been discussing throughout this study.

The force of these allusions to "his wrath" (cf. how *"hamato"* is tied to *"abeit-galuto"* in xi.6 above), "cup", and "destroying him" (*teval'enu*) is turned against "the Wicked Priest" in xi.14f. Since the thrust of the allusion to the Lord's "cup of wrath" is one of divine vengeance and retribution for the destruction of the Righteous Teacher[44] (as the *pesher* itself puts the proposition in the next section referring to the destruction of "the Poor": "as he himself criminally conspired to destroy the Poor, so will God condemn him to destruction"/"he shall be paid the reward which he himself tendered the Poor"), the sense of *"teval'enu"* here, and as a consequence that of *"leval'o"*/*"leval'am"* earlier, is certainly that of "destruction"—in this instance divine destruction. In xi.13f. the phrase "walking in his Way of satiation" or "in the Way of drinking his fill" is usually translated in terms of alleged "drunkenness" on the part of the Wicked Priest. But the allusion has nothing whatever to do with "drunkenness" except figuratively (in the sense of "drinking the cup of his own" or "the Lord's wrath"—a mistake typical of the approach of Qumran research to these matters). Rather it parodies the proper "Zadokite" stress on "walking in the Way of Uprightness" or "Perfection of the Way" and relates to the "cup" and "wrath" imagery in the underlying text in continuation of the theme of violent retribution. It expresses how the Wicked Priest, in "sating" his "own wrath" upon the Righteous Teacher (xi.5f.) would himself taste from the "cup" of the

---

[44] Cf. 4QpPs 37,ii.12ff. and iv.7ff. *N.b.*, here the *'Arizei-Go'im* take vengeance for the Righteous Teacher who has already been violently done to death by the Wicked Priest. As noted, we identify these *'Arizei-Go'im* (who are not necessarily the same as the *'Arizim* in the *pesher*) with those renegade Herodian "Men-of-War" like Silas, Niger of Perea, and Philip son of Jacimus, all formerly intimates of Agrippa II, who first support the uprising and are later either consumed by or desert it. One should also note that in this *pesher* the Man of Lying once again "leads Many astray with words of Lies" (*Sheker*; i.18f.), God executes Judgement (*Mishpat*) on the Wicked Priest through "the hands of the Violent Ones of the Gentiles" (ii.21; in our view identical with Josephus' mysterious "Idumaeans"), and "Lebanon" imagery also occurs (iv.13).

Lord's divine "wrath" (xi.14; cf. Re 14:10 on "His cup of anger" in precisely this vein).

The idea that the Wicked Priest "*criminally* conspired to destroy the Poor" (italics mine—"*zamam lechalot Ebionim*") adds a more indirect or "judicial" dimension, as we have noted, to these "*leval^co*"/"*leval^cam*" charges (therefore perhaps their seeming obscurity). We have already placed James at the center of difficulties in the Temple between "Zealots" (cf. Acts 21:21 on the majority of James' "Jerusalem Church" supporters) and "Herodians", particularly where so-called "gifts from foreigners" were concerned. The meaning of "*zamam*" is completely in keeping with that "conspiracy" we mentioned above between Agrippa II and Ananus to effect the removal of James. But it also carries another more "judicial" sense relating to "bearing false witness" or "perjury", which brings us back to Josephus' picture of the Sanhedrin proceedings Ananus "pursued" against James and his companions and is particularly appropriate to Josephus' report that "the most equitable citizens" protested against the "breach of the Law" implicit in them. If we now view the phrase, "*be-cha^cas hamato abeit-galuto*" ("with *his* angry wrath at *his* house of exile"—italics mine), in the context of these proceedings, apply it *to Ananus, not James* (*i.e.* "the *beit*-expletive" of Ananus), then "*abeit-galuto*" can be seen as an insulting circumlocution relating to these proceedings which the sectaries would not dignify with the title of either a "*beit-din*" or "*beit-mishpat*". The whole then translates more logically: "The Wicked Priest...pursued the Righteous Teacher to destroy him in *his* hot anger in *his* guilty trial" (italics mine). It is certainly remarkable that, when the obscurity surrounding such notices is parted only a little, so much good sense can be made of them in the context even of *known* historical events and traditions relating to James.

The text now draws to a close with an analysis that turns on references to "the violence done to Lebanon", "the destruction of the dumb beasts", and "the violence done to the land" in the underlying text (Hab 2:17). The allusion to "Lebanon" also is to be found in the ambiance of the Is 3:10 materials applied to James' death in early Church tradition. It is subjected to exegesis in several other Qumran documents, most notably 4QpIs^a on Is 10:33f.[45] In Qumran exposition, it almost always carries an esoteric sense connected to a play on the root meaning of "white" relating either to the Community Council or the Temple (ac-

---

[45] Cf. 1QpHab,xii.2ff. with 4QpIs^c on 14:8ff. and on Zech 11:11/Is 30:1ff., 4QpNah,i.7, and 4QpIs^a on 10:33f. That in these various Qumran contexts the expression "Lebanon" is interpreted to variously mean, the Community Council, the Temple, etc., should not be too surprising in view of the identification of the Council with the Temple in the context of spiritualized atonement imagery in 1QS,viii.1ff.

cording to 1QS metaphor and to a certain extent Paul in 1 Co above these are, in effect, the same). This play-on-words parallels that already encountered in the Qumran exegesis of "Zadok"/"*Zaddik*" and its further extensions in *Moreh ha-Zedek* and Melchizedek. Here, however, the text unhesitatingly (as in the case of *Zaddik* with *Moreh ha-Zedek* at the beginning of the *pesher*) identifies "Lebanon" as "the Council of the Community" (xii.4f.). Not only does this mean the one at Qumran, but in our view that of 'the Jerusalem Church' as well. In 4QpIs^a, although the text is somewhat damaged, "Lebanon" appears to represent the Temple and/or priestly establishment, but there also appears to be some mention of the community in the form of "the Poor" (here *Dallim/^cAnavei-Arez*) amid a barrage of Messianic imagery.[46] In 4QpIs^c on Is 14:8, "Lebanon" again appears to be the Community Council, while on Zech 11:11/Is 30:1-5 we have a parallel to one of the classic Talmudic references to the 70 C.E. fall of the Temple.[47]

Not only is it implied that the Wicked Priest *destroyed* the Community Council, *i.e.*, "he shall be paid the reward which he himself tendered to

---

[46] The allusion to "Lebanon" in Is 10:34 is followed by the famous "Messianic" material in 11:1ff. This is interpreted in strict Messianic manner as relating to "the branch of David who will arise at the end of days", smite the earth with the rod of his mouth, and judge all peoples with his sword. "Arise", here, is a translation of the Hebrew, *ha-^camod*, "who will stand up". If we are correct in considering this usage to carry something of the sense of "be resurrected" in the Zadokite Document, then this exegesis coincides even more closely with parallel notions known to early Christianity. An alternate translation would, therefore, run something like: "At the end of days, the branch of David will be resurrected and judge the Poor and the Meek with Righteousness, etc". In addition to Lam.R,ii.3.6, see xxiv of the prologue applying this very word "*^camod*" to the "Messianic" return of Moses.

[47] See *ARN* 4, where in the context of delineating R. Yohanan's attempt to recommend himself as a "friend" to the Emperor (*n.b.*, the similar legend, "friend of Caesar" or "friend of the Romans", on the coins of Herod of Chalcis and his son Aristobulus the husband of Herodias' daughter Salome in this period—Agrippa I even published himself, not without a little hyperbole, as "King Agrippa Great Lover of Caesar"), "Lebanon" is emphatically interpreted in terms of the fall of the Temple in 70 C.E. The two passages cited in this regard, Is 10:34 and Zech 11:1, both find their parallels in extant Qumran materials; cf. 4QpIs^c on Zech 11:11/Is 30:1ff. For additional Talmudic references of this nature, see b. Gitt 56a including Is 10:33f. and b. Yoma 39b including Zech 11:1 and Nah 1:4. For more general references see b. Yoma 21a. There is no indication that these passages were ever applied to a fall of the Temple prior to 70 C.E. Curiously, it would appear that 4QpIs^c on Is 14:8ff. was also about to refer to Zechariah, but Allegro did not attempt a reconstruction. There also appears in Is 30:3 a reference to *Ma^coz* ("Strength" or "Fortress"), a title used in 1QH to refer to the redeeming activities of its author (probably the teacher himself), and probably not unrelated to James' title of *Oblias*, again in early Church literature "Protection of the People" or "Fortress". Here, too, however, the *pesher* is missing. Is 14:30 makes the ritual reference to the *Ebionim* and *Dallim*, but the exegesis here is also missing. *Ebionim, Zaddik, ma^casim* ("works"), *beit-Ya^cacov* ("House of Jacob"); cf. materials surrounding the *zaddik*-passage in Is 3:10 that early Church literature applied to the death of James referring to "*beit-Ya^cacov*" and "Lebanon") etc. also appear in another fragment of 4QpIs^c on Is 29:19ff.

the Poor'', for which ''God would condemn him (the Wicked Priest) to destruction'' (here expressed quite straightforwardly as ''*lechalah*''; xii.2ff.), but the ambiance is also that of the earlier ''robbing the Poor of their substance'' (xii.10). Not only did ''the Priest'' ''criminally conspire to destroy the Poor'' (including the note of ''juridical intrigue'' and/or ''criminal conspiracy'' discussed above), he is even said to have ''defiled the Temple of God''. As with regard to the problems circulating about the person of James, to which it is related, we have already placed this notice about ''polluting the Temple'' within the context of the controversy over admitting Herodians into the Temple and accepting gifts from foreigners and noted the constant reiteration of a parallel theme in the sections of the *War* leading up to Josephus' description of the demise of Ananus.[48] As one of the two main sins (the second is ''*To'evot*''—the ''Abominations'' of his treatment of the Righteous Teacher and ''destruction of the Poor'') for which the Wicked Priest is condemned, it cannot be underestimated. It is also reflected in the Zadokite Document's ''three nets of Belial'' charges against the Jerusalem establishment (the other two, it should be remembered, were *Riches* and *marrying nieces/divorce*, all with particular relevance where Herodians were concerned). It also relates to the ''separation''/''pollution of the Temple'' materials, invoking ''*balla'*'' or ''*Bela'*'' in 11QT,xlvif.

There can be little doubt that in this section of the Habakkuk *Pesher*, as in quite a few elsewhere in the *pesharim*, the term *Ebionim*, applied in early Church usage to ''Jewish Christians'' (and by Paul to 'the Jerusalem Church'), is specifically being applied by the community to itself. Punctuating the point, it is employed three times in this section, though it nowhere appears in the underlying text of Habakkuk.[49] However '*Ani*, one of its parallels, probably best translated by the New Testament's ''the Meek'', does appear in Hab 3:14 and occurs in close proximity to the Is 3:10 passage which early Church testimony applies to the circumstances of James' death. '*Ani/'Anavim* also appears together with another parallel *Dallim* in the Is 10:33f. ''Lebanon'' passage above. Like *Ebion/Ebionim* it is widespread in Qumran usage and sometimes even coupled with *Ebion*.[50] In this section of the *pesher*, the *Ebionim* are iden-

---

[48] See War 4.2.3ff. particularly 4.3.2, 4.3.7ff., 4.3.11, 4.3.13, 4.4.3, 4.5.2, etc. One should appreciate that the imagery, which also includes reference to ''Traitors'' and the like, as one would expect and parallel to the methodology of the New Testament, is usually inverted.

[49] 1QpHab,xii.3 (again in conjunction with allusion to ''Lebanon''), xii.6, and xii.10.

[50] See Hab 3:14; cf., as well Zech 11:7 and 11:11—the actual passage subjected to exegesis in 4QpIs^c, Is 3:14f. in proximity to the Is 3:10 passage above, and Is 14:29f. already noted in 4QpIs^c above. See also Is 10:21ff. in 4QpIs^c on ''the remnant of Jacob'', which includes references to ''the Poor'' and ''Lebanon''; cf. as well, similar combinations of *Ebion* and '*Ani* in CD,vi.21 and xiv.13. For *nephesh-Ebion* and *nephesh-'Ani*, both synonyms for the usage *nephesh-Zaddik* in Is 53:11 (and CD,i.20), see 1QH,ii.32ff., iii.25, and v.18ff.

tified with another group called "the Simple Ones of Judah doing *Torah*" (*Peta'ei*-Yehudah *'oseh ha-Torah*).

This latter euphemism, not only should be understood in terms of expressions in the New Testament like "these Little Ones" and "the *'Anavei-Arez*" in 4QpIs[a] 15 above, but it occurs not insignificantly twice in an environment of familiar allusions to being "misled"/"led astray" and "joining" in 4QpNah,iii.5 and 7. In the first it is connected with the "Ephraim" circumlocution, *i.e.*, "the Simple Ones of Ephraim (*n.b.* the significant omission of xii.4f.'s *'oseh ha-Torah* when speaking about these "*Peta'ei*-Ephraim") will forsake...those who mislead them and join themselves (*nilvu*) to Israel". The reference to "*nilvu*" is crucial and clinches the entire presentation. Not only is it linked to the use of the parallel expression "*nilvim*" in Es 10:27 as expressive of Gentiles "attaching themselves" to the Jewish Community (cf. the use of "*ger-nilveh*" carrying this sense in 4QpNah,ii.9) and in the *esoteric* exegesis of the Zadokite Covenant in CD,iv.3, but once again it brings all these imageries full circle providing *definitive confirmation* of the correctness of our original identification of "Ephraim" as Gentile God-fearers "misled"/"led astray" by a more antinomian Pauline teacher. By linking these "Simple of Ephraim" with "the Seekers after Smooth Things...at the end of Time", the Nahum *Pesher* also provides support for our other historical thesis concerning the generic thrust of the latter usage as implying all "those seeking accommodation with foreigners", and that originally Qumran sectaries saw so-called "Pharisees" and "Pauline Christians" as part and parcel of the same alliance. Such evidence from a third independent textual context (in addition to that of 1QpHab and CD) provides important verification of what might have appeared on the surface a speculative suggestion and confirms as nothing else can the accuracy of our categorization of the "Ephraim" usage as relating *inter alia* to *Pauline Christians*.

Returning to the context of the Habakkuk *Pesher*, one can specify with a fair degree of precision that "the Poor" and "the Simple Ones" ("of Judah", not Ephraim), as used in xii.3ff., are more or less coequal appellations, except "the Poor" is a little more general and meant to include the Community Council or leadership as well. Conversely, "the Simple of Judah doing *Torah*", like the parallel "*'Osei ha-Torah*" in vii.11 and viii.1, probably was not meant to include the leadership as such, but rather only the rank and file—the beneficiaries of the justifying activities of the Council/Central Triad/Righteous Teacher in 1QS,viiiff. and 1QpHab,viii above. For the *pesher*, "the dumb beasts" who are *destroyed* in the underlying text are "the Simple of Judah doing *Torah*". By implication, too, as in the exegesis both of Hab 2:3 and 2:4 above, the exegete wants us to understand that *they are not* "the Simple Ones" (cf. the term "Little Ones" in the N.T.) not of "Judah", *i.e.*, not *non-Jews*—in the terms of the Nahum *Pesher*, not "the Simple Ones of Ephraim" unless they had in some prior manner specifically "joined" themselves to "Israel" or "the House of Judah" (cf. *ʿam ʿim ger-nilveh* in 4QpNah,ii.9).

This theme of "destruction" in the underlying text is applied in the exegesis to "the Poor", including and not exclusive of the community leadership, for which the Wicked Priest was to be specifically "condemned (by God) to destruction" (xii.5ff.). This last note links the exegesis directly with that of the "cup" of divine retribution and the plural destruction of the Righteous Teacher and some of his followers in xi preceding it, already considered above. As used in xii.4f. above, "the Simple of Judah *doing Torah*" (italics mine) establishes a perfect and purposeful contrast with xii.8's description of the "acts" or "works" of the Wicked Priest as "*maʿasei-Toʿevot*" ("works of Abominations"). Since the latter usage is attached to the notice about "polluting the Temple of God" (xii.9), which we have also considered above, it is meant to be recapitulative of the earlier "Ways of *Toʿevot*... in all unclean *tumʾah*" in which the Wicked Priest *acted* "to heap guilt on himself" in viii.12f. The *pesher* also relates this usage to "the violence done to the land", etc. in the underlying text, which it will now proceed to interpret in terms of "robbing the Poor" in the villages round about Jerusalem and the destruction of the Teacher and some members of his Council. As noted above, we have already encountered the signification "doing-*Torah*" (*ʿoseh ha-Torah*) in the exposition of Hab 2:4, where those who "would be saved" by their faith in the *Zaddik/Moreh ha-Zedek* were specified as "*Torah*-Doers in the House of Judah" (meant also, as we can now see, to contrast with the "House of Ephraim"). In the exegesis of Hab 2:3 on "the delay of the *Parousia*" preceding it, these "*Torah*-Doers" were instructed to wait patiently. Ja 5:7 (which earlier in 1:22ff. had addressed itself to these same "Doers") counsels a similar eschatological patience under similar circumstances, and Ja 5:3's note about "gold and silver... in the last days" will now reappear in the underlying text from Hab 2:19f. about to be expounded in the concluding eschatological exegesis about the "Day of Judgement" in xiii.1ff.

For xii.7f. the Community Council is actually functioning in this period in Jerusalem, not Qumran, since "Jerusalem" is straightforwardly designated as the locale "where the Wicked Priest committed his abominable acts" against it (as well as "polluting the Temple"). Consequently, this "*ʿAzat ha-Yahad*" must be considered virtually indistinguishable from what goes in other contexts by the name of either "the Jerusalem Council" or "the Jerusalem Church". Again these kinds of "abominable acts" are meant to contrast with those "Righteous" ones or *maʿasei-Torah* predicated of the Righteous Teacher and so much a part of the ideological approach of the Letter of James. To summarize: "As he himself criminally conspired to destroy the Poor", *i.e.*, "in Jerusalem where (he) ... committed his acts of abomination" and in "the cities of Judah where he robbed the Poor of their substance"[51]; so too would the Wicked Priest "be paid the reward which he himself tendered the Poor" and "be condemned (by God) to destruction".[52] That what is implied here is nothing other than the reward the Wicked Priest paid the Righteous Teacher and the members of his Council is also clear in the passage from Hab 2:17 underlying the exegesis:

> For the violence done to Lebanon shall overwhelm you and the destruction of the dumb beasts shall brand you because of the blood of men and the violence done to the land, the city, and all its inhabitants.

Here, "Lebanon" is specifically identified as "the Community Council"; "the violence done to Lebanon" is the stoning of James and some of his associates in 62 C.E. as reported in Josephus and variously reflected in early Church sources—the "whitening" imagery purposely evoking the *white linen* they wore and their purported sinlessness; "the dumb beasts" are "the Simple Jews" or "the *Ebionim* of Jerusalem" variously referred to as "Jewish Christians", "the Jerusalem Church", and referred to in Ro 15:26, 16:18, Ga 2:10, Ja 2:2ff. etc.; "the blood of men" (here the allusion is real and is overtly so designated in the *pesher* because we are speaking about the rapine and murder remounting *directly* to the Wicked Priest, not the Spouter of Lying) refers once again to James and his associates on the Community Council (cf. ix.9ff. above); and "the violence done to the land", etc., is the "polluting the Temple" both with the violence done to James and others and by admitting and accepting gifts from *Herodians* and other foreigners along with the concomitant robbing of the tithes of the poor priests in the cities of Judea outside Jerusalem so vividly described in Josephus' several references.[53]

---

[51] 1QpHab,xii.9f. See above, pp. 22 and 43f. for how the servants of the high priests robbed "the Poor" among the lower priests of their tithes and the reflection of this in the so-called "Zealot woes".

[52] 1QpHab,xii.5ff.; the "abominable works" (*maʿasei-Toʿevot*) of the Wicked Priest referred to in xii.8 are the counterpart of the "Righteous" ones, or the *maʿasei-Zedek* of the teacher whom he destroys; cf. how the same terminologies, "abomination" (relating to his "violence") and "pollution" (relating to his Temple desecration) are reflected in the earlier description of "the Ways" of the Wicked Priest in viii.12f. These themes of "*Toʿevot*" (Abominations) and "*tumʾa*" (pollution) also dominate the Temple Scroll.

[53] It is clear from the context that some of the members of the Council (referred to as well here as "the Poor") share the fate of the Righteous Teacher; cf. *Ant* 20.9.1 where James and some others close to him are all condemned to death. This was, of course,

Where the "Lebanon shall fall by a mighty one" allusion is concerned in 4QpIs[a], one encounters many themes even in the extant text paralleling those of Hab 1-2, including the conquest by oncoming *Kittim*, the allusions to the "Meek", "Downtrodden", etc., together with an additional one, "the rising of David at the end of days" (including the use of the telltale "*ʿamod*", i.e., "standing up") in a similar, if albeit fragmentary, exegesis. Even more significantly, however, as in the case of the exegesis of Hab 2:4, we have incontrovertible evidence from independent sources, in this instance Talmudic, that this "Lebanon" passage in Is 10:33f. *was* being subjected to exegesis in the latter part of the first century and *was* applied to the fall of the Temple in 70 C.E. The same is true of Zech 11:11/Is 30:1-5.[54] Whether the exegesis of these passages

stated explicitly in ix.9ff. The whole exegesis is paralleled in 4QpPs 37, which also combines repeated allusions to the *Zaddik/Zaddikim* with the *ʿAnavim, Ebionim, Tamimim,* Lebanon, *Maʿoz*, etc. As in 1QpHab, the Community Council is described as "doing the Law" (*ʿoseh ha-Torah*, with an accent on "doing"; ii.22), and it is clear that they (referred to as well as "the Community of the Poor") share to a certain extent the fate of the teacher —here, also, referred to as "the Priest", *i.e.*, "the high priest". The sentence, "the Wicked watches out for the Righteous and seeks to slay him," in 4QpPs 37,ii.12 and iv.7 is completely paralleled by 1QpHab,i.11f., CD,i.20f. (*n.b.* at this point the Zadokite Document is stringing together materials from Is 30 and a *zaddik*-allusion from Ps 94:21), and Is 3:10. In so far as the *ʿArizei-Goʾim* ("Violent Ones of the Gentiles") in 4QpPs 37,ii.21 and iv.10 are to be identified with the *ʿArizim* in the Habakkuk *Pesher*, they also must be connected, as we have seen, with the Lying Spouter and "Covenant-Breaking". In 1QpHab,ii.6 the *ʿArizim* are described "as not believing what they heard from the mouth of the Priest" concerning the last times, *i.e.*, they were privy to his exegeses. As we have seen in n. 44 above, they are to be identified with quite a few Herodian Men-of-War, including "Niger", "Silas", "Philip", even Queen Helen's son Monobazus, who along with "John the Essene" are among the uprising's bravest military commanders; cf. *War* 2.20.4 and 3.2.1. Niger the Peraite is an important leader of Josephus' "Idumaeans" (according to our interpretation, pro-revolutionary "Herodians") who are seen by the exegete as the instruments of God's retribution on Ananus. Niger is finally caught up in factional division and undergoes public execution at the hands of the revolutionary crowds, the atmosphere surrounding which (perhaps not completely coincidentally) is very similar to that portrayed in the New Testament surrounding the execution of Jesus.

[54] In the fragment relating to Is 14:8-30, once again one has "Lebanon" mentioned in the context of a reference to the *Dallim* and *Ebionim* which seems to have so appealed to the sectaries. In fact if one makes a list of the incidences of these kinds of words in the Prophets and Psalms, one will find that one has probably inadvertently stumbled on the actual method used by Qumran exegetes in choosing scriptural texts. "Lebanon" is to be found in Is 2:13 (in proximity to the 3:10 material applied to James' death), 10:34, 14:8, 29:17, 33:9, 35:2, 37:24, 40:16, 60:13, Nah 1:4, Zech 10:10, 11:1, and Hab 2:17. The words, "Poor" and "Meek", either represented by *Ebion*, *ʿAni*, or *Dal*, are to be found in Is 3:14f., 10:2, 10:30, 11:4, 14:30f., 25:4ff., 29:19, 32:7, 41:17, 58:7, 66:2, and Zech 11:7ff. Almost every one of these passages where the two usages have been found in conjunction has been subjected to exegesis in extant materials at Qumran. If we include the Is 3:10 passage known to have been subjected to exegesis with regard to the events of James' life, then the passages where such correspondences occur are virtually exhausted. (should an Is 3:10 *pesher* prove extant among the unpublished fragments from Cave IV of Qumran, this would constitute additional strong verification of our position.)

parallels the Talmudic in *every* respect is not the crucial issue (nor is it where Pauline exegesis of Hab 2:4 is concerned) and impossible to say in all cases because of the imperfect preservation of some *pesharim*. What is, however, important is that "Lebanon" imagery *was being* associated with the fall of the Temple in 70 C.E. There is not the slightest evidence from any other source that exegesis of this kind was applied to any previous fall of the Temple, or, as we have emphasized, that such exegesis was even being practised prior to about 30 C.E. in any systematic manner, *i.e.*, roughly the time of the appearance of "the Messianic Movement" and the last stage of period II of Qumran habitation. In the face of such persuasive historical and textual evidence for the *sitz-im-leben* of the Habakkuk *Pesher*, one must be able to present substantive evidence from another source to controvert it, but this cannot be done (nor should one expect in the face of the numerous connections to events of this period we have already been able to show that it could be done).

The *pesher* ends poignantly (in view of the historical circumstances which form its *sitz-im-leben*) and appropriately enough, in terms of the ideological concerns and internecine disputes which characterized its previous subject matter, with an outright and fulsome condemnation of all "Gentiles" (*Goʾim*) and "the idols they serve" (xii.12ff.). We are to understand that these "idols" include, not only those "served" by the present destroyers of Jerusalem and the Temple, *i.e.*, the Romans (including their omnipresent standards), but also that "idolatry" implicit in the Spouter's "Lying" activities and in the acceptance of sacrifices and gifts on behalf of Herodians (considered here as Gentiles) and other foreigners in the Temple. These "idols" would "not be able to save them on the Day of Judgement" (*Yom ha-Mishpat*). The use of the verb "*yazzilum*" here is purposeful. It parallels the use of "*yazzilem*" in the earlier Hab 2:4 exegesis reversing its signification because it is now talking about "idolatrous Gentiles" not "*Torah*-Doing Jews". It also provides *absolute confirmation* that our initial characterization of the earlier use of "*yazzilem*" in the *pesher* (and by implication the use of the mysterious "*Beit ha-Mishpat*" connected to it) as *eschatological* was correct, because in the present textual context the use of "*yazzilum*" and the "*Yom ha-Mishpat*", to which it is tied, are undoubtedly eschatological. Just as in viii.1ff. it was only "the Doers of *Torah*" in "the House of Judah" whom God "would save" from "the House of Judgement", here all idolatrous "Gentiles" are being condemned (as well as—as we shall see in xiii.4—"backsliding Jews").

The use, too, of the word "*leʿovdam*", "to serve them", in xii.13 and its slightly varied repetition in xiii.2's "served" and xiii.3's "Servants", is also not without a touch of irony. It is of particular import where the presumed idolatrous "city" built upon blood by the Lying Spouter who "tires out Many with worthless work/service (*ʿavodat-shavo*) and teaches them works of Lying" in x.11f. is concerned, and the implications of such usage are fully set forth in the portrait of "the Spirit of *ʿAvlah*... and slackness in the service of Righteousness" in 1QS,iv.9ff. As with the implied parallel between the use of "gold and silver" in the underlying text from Hab 2:18 and the "gold and silver" in the eschatological Judgement section of the Letter of James above, the underlying text from Hab 2:19 also contains a somewhat obscure note about "Lying" (*Sheker*; variously rendered as "teacher of Lying", "Lying images", or the like) which links up with the "*maʿasei-Sheker*" ("acts" or "works of Lying") aspect of the above references.

The allusion to "*Yom ha-Mishpat*" is repeated in the repetition of the condemnation on "all the Gentiles" in the conclusion of the *pesher* (xiii.1ff.) and, because of the parallelism of its language and the sense of the exegesis, completely validates our earlier translation of the phrase "House of Judgement" as synonymous with this "Day of Judgement" (while the former has more the connotation of the actual *decision* of "Judgement", the latter is more connotative of the event itself). The vision of this "Judgement" is broadened to include "idolators" generally, *i.e.* "the Servants of Graven Images" (cf. Paul's contempt for "the Servants of Righteousness" in 2 Co 11:15) and "Evil Ones" generally ("*Reshaʿim*"), which must be seen as inclusive of Jews like the paradigmatic "*Cohen ha-Rashaʿ*" who "betrayed the Law" and/or "Covenant" or who served it "only when convenient". Here the verb used to express this hope for the rendering of such eschatological Judgement in xiii.3, "*yechaleh*", is the same as that "*lechalah*"/"*lechalot*" used in xii.5f. to express the vengeance that God would visit upon the Wicked Priest for his "destruction of the Poor". The inclusion in this "Judgement" of these "*Reshaʿim*" (meaning primarily backsliding *Jews*), in addition to idolatrous Gentiles, completely parallels that "Judgement" which God would pronounce "through the hands of his Elect" on both "the Gentiles" (primarily those *Kittim* presently destroying the land and their "Pauline"/Herodian confreres) and "*the Wicked of his own people who kept the Law only when convenient*" in v.3ff. (italics mine; here too the verb employed to express the withholding of *complete* "destruction" from "his own people" is the usual "*yechaleh*").

The text ends, as with the Letter of James it so much resembles and the earlier discussion of 'the delay of the *Parousia*', on a pious note of quiet confidence, which could not contrast more with the debacle occurring at the present moment, a debacle itself the ostensible reason for its composition. Delivered in exposition of Hab 2:20's equally pious underlying sentiment: "The Lord is in his Holy Temple; let all the earth be still before Him"; it expresses the apocalyptic and, given the *sitz-im-leben*, poignantly optimistic expectation that "on the Day of Judgement God would destroy from off the earth all those serving idols and all the Evil Ones".

CHAPTER THREE

THE ARCHAEOLOGICAL EVIDENCE

We can, as should by now be clear, account in our theory for almost every allusion, every sentence, even almost every turn-of-phrase in the Habakkuk *Pesher*. We can, in addition, put them into *real* historical settings relating to *real* and important people contemporary with the fall of the Temple about 70 C.E. when the scrolls were supposed to have been put into the caves and when parallel exegeses were circulating relating to Hab 2:4 and "Lebanon" imagery in Prophets and Psalms. There is no other theory of Qumran origins or identifications which can achieve as much. What then holds or has held scholars back from arriving at such identifications? Since, where the Habakkuk *Pesher* is concerned, palaeography is not an important issue, aside from an ideological predisposition not to arrive at such results (in some instances even a psychological one), the only real impediment has been the archaeology of Qumran. Even though it, too, was based on many of these same psychological and ideological predispositions, many scholars adhered to this archaeology as if it presented an insurmountable barrier.

If, even accepting the validity of Qumran archaeological theory as it presently stands, one were required to account for the whole expanse of Qumran literature on the basis of our presentation, it would not be difficult. It is possible to identify a series of martyred *"Zaddikim"* beginning with Onias the son of Simeon the *Zaddik*. Judas Maccabee[1], Honi the Circle-Drawer[2], his grandson Hanan the Hidden[3], John the Baptist (if not identical to Hanan the Hidden)[4], Jesus[5], James, etc., are all iden-

---

[1] I have covered the subject of Judas as *Zaddik* in *Maccabees, Zadokites, Christians and Qumran*, pp. 2, 12ff., and 21ff.

[2] We have already discussed Honi the Circle-Drawer above in relation to rain-making. Josephus, calling him "Onias the Just", identifies him (in our view definitively) as a *Zaddik*/"Righteous Man" in *Ant.* 14.2.1. Cf. also b. Taʿan 23a.

[3] We have also discussed Hanan *ha-Nehba* above in relation to rain-making. The "hidden" theme associated with his person was also an element in Josephus' description of his grandfather Onias. This theme is also discernible in Lk 1:24's description of John the Baptist's mother "Elizabeth" who "hid herself" and in the Protevangelium of James 18:1, where Elizabeth "hides" John in a *mountain cave* when Herod tries to escape him. For the *Zohar*, i,63a and 67b, Noah "was hidden" by God in the ark in order to escape both someone it calls "the Adversary" and the impending eschatological flood. Cave-dwelling is also an important theme of both the *"redivivus"* and *"rain-making"* traditions.

[4] John, of course, is identified as a "Righteous One" who "came in the Way of Righteousness" in Mt 21:32 and Mk 6:20; in these accounts it is always foreigners, Herodians, or Roman governors who properly recognize *Zaddikim*. Josephus, too, in his cap-

tified in one way or another as *Zaddikim* in the extant literature. However, in the particular instance of the Habakkuk *Pesher*, recourse to the broader implications of such theorizing is not necessary because the identifications we propose fit very comfortably into the present confines of Qumran archaeological and palaeographic theory and the internal data.[6] Since the advance, as we have emphasized, of "the *Kittim*" and the imminent destruction of "the last priests of Jerusalem" were for the *pesher* events in progress, not necessarily completed, there is no reason why it could not have been written in 68 C.E.

Even more germane for our purposes, most scholars have arrived at a date for the fall of the monastery on the basis of their interpretations of coin data, a fragile tool under the best conditions. The date, however, which they have arrived at for the fall of the monastery and the deposit of the scrolls in the caves (which they envision as simultaneous events) is 68 C.E. But this is not the latest possible date for either of these two events, but simply the earliest one, *i.e.*, it is not a *terminus ad quem*, but a *terminus a quo* (unless these two *termini* are identical which is, of course, the implication of their theories). In particular, if we are talking only about "the fall

---

sule description of John's baptism and death in *Ant.* 18.5.2, implies that John enjoyed such a status. For Josephus, John is teaching what Justin Martyr calls the "all Righteousness" doctrine (cf. Mt 3:15), characterized by the dichotomy of *Hesed* and *Zedek*, *i.e.*, the Piety commandment of "loving God" and the Righteousness commandment of "loving one's neighbor as oneself", the latter evolving into notions of economic equality and poverty. Justin Martyr treats these matters in *Dial.* 23, 47, and 93. Not only do they form the backbone of Josephus' long description of "Essene" doctrine in *War* 2.8.2ff., but also his short note about Essenes in *Ant.* 15.10.5. Josephus also applies these categories to the person of Simeon the *Zaddik* in *Ant* 12.2.5. They are also presented as forming the essence of Jesus' teaching in Mt 22:34ff. and Mk 12:28ff. and are set forth no uncertain terms as "the two Ways" in the first section of the *Didache* 1.1.

[5] Acts refers to Jesus repeatedly as "the Just One" or *Zaddik*. Paul, as we have seen, in 1 Co 15:3, introducing his version of post-resurrection appearances, reveals his familiarity with the "justification" ideal based on the ideology of Is 53:11f. and implies that he learned it in *Jerusalem*. More importantly, Ja 5:4 in discussing matters relating to the Messianic return and the condemnation of "the Rich" leading up to its evocation of eschatological "rain" imagery, knows that "the Just One" was done to death. But unlike Paul in 1 Thess (who blames the Jews), it, probably more accurately, blames *the Rich* for this murder.

[6] Milik, p. 64, categorically placed 1QpHab in the mid or late first century C.E., insisting it "could not come from any part of the first century B.C." We have already noted the range of opinion concerning its "secure" Herodian dating above. On internal data alone, however, including its exegesis of Hab 2.4, its presentation of what generally goes by the name of "the delay of the *Parousia*", its use of the terminology of Is 53:11 in its eschatological exegesis of Hab 2:4, its reference to "the last priests of Jerusalem" in the context of its discussions about the death of the Righteous Teacher, its use of "the Poor" terminology to refer to his community, and its eschatological use of the language of "the last times" and "the Day of Judgement", one can assert with a fair degree of certitude that *Habakkuk is late*.

of the monastery", this date says nothing about the cessation of *Jewish* habitation around the area of the site.[7]

For these purposes, it is important, as we have shown, to distinguish between "cessation of habitation" *at* or *around* and the "destruction of buildings" *on* a given site. Though the buildings at Qumran may have been destroyed in 68 C.E., or even some years later, habitation in the area, particularly at Ein Feshka, did not come to an end until after the Bar Kochba uprising in 136 C.E. The actual *terminus ad quem*, therefore, for the deposit of the scrolls in the caves at Qumran (if not the *destruction* of its buildings) is 136. R. De Vaux, who along with his colleagues J. T. Milik and F. M. Cross, did more than anyone else to establish the consensus that presently surrounds these issues, was sometimes (though not often) willing to admit these technicalities.[8] Despite this, many of his conclusions were rather routinely employed to develop palaeographic sequences which were themselves then used to date documents—in some cases even *in an absolute manner*. Where these sequences and the absolute dates derived from them were concerned, a precision came to be claimed in relation to individual documents in some cases down to within 25 years of the theoretical date of production of that document.[9]

But De Vaux's own work was not always so precise. Sometimes it was even extremely problematic. In his enthusiasm for his proposal of a 68 C.E. *terminus* for the *simultaneous* destruction of the monastery and the deposit of the scrolls in the caves, he announced that he had found a coin bearing the countersign of the Xth Roman Legion.[10] But this proved to

---

[7] This has particular relevance when groups are following a "Rechabite" or "wilderness" life-style as at Qumran.

[8] De Vaux, to his credit, states, p. 41: "It is perfectly true that strictly speaking the coins only provide a *terminus post quem*"; but sometimes he drops his diplomatic approach and states categorically, as on p. 112: "The community installed itself at Qumran in the second half of the second century B.C. It abandoned the site for a period of some thirty years during the reign of Herod the Great, and definitively left the area in A.D. 68." No wonder the greater part of his followers take this for a *terminus ad quem* and not the *terminus post quem* he admits it is above. Here Cross in "The Oldest Manuscripts from Qumran", *SBL*, 1955, p. 163, has accurately understood that the "absolute *terminus ad quem* for Qumran script types" are the dated documents from the Wadi Murabba'at (though sometimes he behaves as if he doesn't). As opposed to this, see Birnbaum, p. 27, quoted above: "Archaeological evidence confirms the post-Christian era part, and even enables us to arrive at a precise *terminus ad quem*: the year 68 C.E., when the Romans put an end to Qumran settlement." Having said this, he then proceeds to plug this date into all his "equations" (such as they are) as the *absolute* upper pole limit for Qumran script types.

[9] See, for instance, Birnbaum, pp. 115ff., where he is willing to project dates down to actual years, corroborates one set of dates by others, and projects new dates on the basis of his previous projections without a word about margins of error.

[10] R. De Vaux, "Fouille au Khirbet Qumran," *Revue Biblique*, 61, 1954, pp. 232f.; he reiterated this claim in *RB*, 63, 1956, p. 567, where he typically treats the conquest and occupation of the site "by the soldiers of the X[e] Legion" as a proven fact. See also Cross,

be inaccurate and later he had to admit that it was not a coin of the Xth
Roman Legion as he had thought and that "such a coin never in fact existed". His retraction, delivered only in a footnote however, never made
the same popular impression as his original announcement.[11] He was
also in large measure responsible for propounding the famous "earthquake hypothesis" to explain the destruction by fire and a seeming inter-
ruption of Qumran settlement during the Herodian period. However,
natural phenomena like Josephus' 31 B.C.E. earthquake are not sufficient to explain this destruction and relative abandonment, for if the sectaries could have returned in 4 B.C.E. (as most commentators theorize),
they could also have returned in 30 or 29 B.C.E., and there must have
been *other* factors (in our view political ones) coinciding with Herod's
reign in Palestine which made habitation at Qumran difficult, if not impossible.

In fact for the perspicacious observer, Josephus explains these quite
straightforwardly in *Ant* 15.10.4 (in the same notice where he discusses
Herod's cordial relation with "Pollio the Pharisee and Sameas and their
community of scholars"). Noting that Herod "greatly guarded against
those malcontents" who objected to "the practices he had introduced into their religion to the dissolution of their customs" (*n.b.*, how Josephus
here reverses the language of "Innovators" and "innovations" which he
will presently apply to those unalterably opposed to the Herodian monar-
chy), Josephus describes how Herod relentlessly persecuted such persons, because they "could in no way be reduced to acquiesce to his
regime." Aside from a ban on public and communal meetings, he set
"spies everywhere, both in the city and on the roads who watched those
that met together." He "watched everything they did, and when any
were caught they were severely punished and many were brought to the
citadel Hyrcania (not far from Qumran) both openly and in secret and
there put to death."

This is all presented in the context of his first description of any consequence of both "Pharisees" and "Essenes". What Josephus has done,
by placing in conjunction parallel notices about Herod's equal regard for
these two groups, as we have suggested elsewhere,[12] is confused them
with each other. The *real* political stance of those "Essenes" responsible

pp. 62ff., particularly n. 18, for detailed analyses of the movements of this legion; also De
Vaux, pp. 38ff. For the opposing view, see C. Roth, "Did Vespasian Capture Qumran",
Palestine Exploration Quarterly, pp. 122ff.

[11] De Vaux, p. 40: "Recent discussions refer to the existence of a coin with the
countersign of the Tenth legion, which, so it is held (by whom?), was found at Khirbet
Qumran and which I have in fact recorded... The mention of this was unfortunate for this
coin does not exist."

[12] *Maccabees, Zadokites, Christians and Qumran*, pp. 45, 53, 55, 58, etc.

for the Qumran corpus may be surmised from his earlier notes about "malcontents...opposing the dissolution of their customs" which introduces these details and is in every way consonant with what we know of Qumran. This *simple historical* error led to quite a few derivative ones which have prevented Qumran commentators from accurately approaching the materials before them. Primarily it gave rise to the notion that "Herod held these Essenes in such honor that he thought higher of them than their mortal nature required" (the group Josephus really intends here are *"Pharisees"* not "Essenes"). This, in turn, has given rise to the common impression that so-called "Essenes" were peace-loving and a rather retiring group with little or no political interests, an impression that has no relationship, as should be obvious, to the apocalyptic spirit and lust for vengeance against political and religious opponents which, as we have seen, permeates the Habakkuk *Pesher*. The practitioners of 1QpHab's "Day of Judgement" (on "all Gentiles", "idolators", and "backsliders") and "Judgement executed at the hands of God's Elect" (resembling nothing so much as the spirit of militancy one encounters in the Koran with its parallel and derivative pronouncements against "idolators" and "backsliders" and its use of the very same "Day of Judgement" terminology throughout) were completely and by definition *anti-Herodian*.

The note about Herod's "innovations to the dissolution of their customs" precisely corresponds to Josephus' later accusations against "Innovators" and the "innovations" sought by those who wished *to ban foreigners from the Temple Mount* (which, as we noted, Josephus typically *reverses*, much as the New Testament "reverses" the ideological orientation and historical drift characterizing Qumran documents in constructing its portrait of similar events). The "innovations" in question are made quite clear in the Zadokite Document's ban on "divorce" and "marrying nieces", as well as its complaints about "pollution of the Sanctuary" already dealt with above. In our view, these were unquestionably aimed directly and unerringly at "Herodians". If the Zadokite Document were the second (even the third century) B.C.E. document most commentators claim (which we dispute categorically—on *textual* grounds not *palaeographic*), this would make Herod's esteem for purported "Essenes" all the more incomprehensible. In fact, the so-called "Essenes" at Qumran (despite these notices in Josephus) *never* approved of "Herodians", which is precisely the reason for both the New Testament's and Josephus' parallel ideological and historical surgeries. It is these historical confusions, misconceptions, and inaccuracies which have, more than anything else, sapped the work of both palaeographers and archaeologists in Qumran studies.

S. Steckoll, whom De Vaux contemptuously dismissed as "this Sherlock Holmes of archaeology",[13] questioned even whether there was evidence of earthquake damage at Qumran. That an earthquake could have caused the kind of complete conflagration that seems to have occurred at Qumran is not very convincing. Even De Vaux's own colleague Milik, who questioned the former's evidence for a total abandonment of the site between 31 B.C.E. and 4 B.C.E., admitted that the evidence of a conflagration was of such magnitude as to suggest "an intentional destruction of Qumran".[14] In any event, since the sectaries do not appear to have inhabited *the buildings* at Qumran, an earthquake, whether it damaged them or not, cannot be used as a measure for the date of the abandonment of the site (the same point applies to the destruction of these *buildings* by Roman soldiers). There are very good reasons for the abandonment of the site coinciding with the period of Herod's reign in Palestine, or at least a severe diminution in the numbers of persons residing there, as we have seen, but in order to appreciate them one must firm up one's *historical* grasp and not be deceived by Josephus' portrait of the Essenes as pro-Herodian. Simply put, the sect was vehemently, even violently, anti-Herodian, and the site was most likely destroyed in 37 B.C.E. by Herod himself on his way up to invest Jerusalem.[15]

Milik and De Vaux have also disagreed with each other on whether the ruins of a wall and the broken dishes which appear to be connected to it appertain to the mid-first century B.C.E. or the destruction in the later part of the first century C.E.[16] Despite the fact that their disagreement in dating such a relatively large piece of masonry amounts to a difference of approximately 100 years, Qumran stratigraphers regularly claim a precision where dating is concerned that comes down in some instances to the month and year, a confidence paralleling that of Qumran palaeographers

---

[13] De Vaux, p. 48. Cf. S. Steckoll, "Marginal Notes on the Qumran Excavations", *Revue de Qumran*, 7, 1968, pp. 34ff.

[14] Cf. Milik, pp. 51ff. Even De Vaux in his last work took a much more conciliatory stance on the subject: "The question remains open, therefore, and my *real reason* for *believing* that the fire coincided with the earthquake of 31 B.C. is that this solution *is the simplest* and that there are *no positive arguments to contradict it*" (*sic*—italics mine).

[15] See for instance Josephus' account in this period of the "Zealot" suicide of the "old man" and his seven sons (whom Josephus refers to as "robbers" 100 years before Masada) in Qumran-type terrain not far from the Jordan valley; *Ant.* 14.15.4f. This episode would appear to have had a certain amount of importance since it has received its fictional refurbishment in the "Eleazar" and the "Seven Brothers" stories in 2 and 4 Macc, which are further refined via *Gematria* in the "Taxo" materials in As Mos 9:1ff. The "Resurrection" ideal, so important to these materials, has received its ultimate parody in Mk 12:20ff./Lk 20:29ff./Mt 22:25ff. That this suicide ideal in this period was part and parcel of the recommendation to "make a pious end" *is confirmed* in the "Razis" material in 2 Macc 14:37ff. See also Appendix on the "three nets of Belial."

[16] See Milik, pp. 51ff., in particular, p. 55, n. 1, and De Vaux, pp. 24ff.

(to which, of course, it is related).[17] Where coins are the issue, one is entitled to say certain kinds of general things based on the general trends of Qumran coin distribution, like the community was founded around the time of John Hyrcanus, or there seems to have been an increase in habitation during the time of Agrippa I, and an even greater one during the Revolt, but one is *not permitted* to make the kinds of precise dating claims that are common to this field. For instance, even if the sect's communal buildings were destroyed in 68 C.E., one cannot *be sure* that habitation in the area of the site then *completely* ceased or that the Romans *in fact* garrisoned the location at this time and not several years later.

De Vaux, Cross, *et al.* point to the non-Jewish coins found at the site overlaying the layer of destruction which they presume to be 68 C.E.[18] However, finding a certain coin at a particular site, as they well know, says nothing about the identity of the person who dropped it there, or for that matter the precise date on which it was dropped, only that it could not have been dropped *before* the date on the coin. Neither does it say anything about the even more important subject of habitation *in the caves* and when they were abandoned, since the inhabitants, as we have noted, do not seem to have lived in the actual buildings of the monastery, but in "Rechabite"-style huts or in the caves themselves. Nor do they appear to have carried any coins on their persons, as no coins of any kind have yet been found in any of the caves.[19] Nor can it say anything, in these circumstances, about when a given cave like Cave 1, where the Habakkuk *Pesher* was found so neatly deposited, was ultimately abandoned.[20] In any

---

[17] Cf. R. North's criticism of De Vaux in "Qumran and its Archaeology", *CBQ*, 16, pp. 426-37 and Milik above. Where stratigraphy is concerned, we are speaking of small coins purportedly suspended between stratigraphic layers. It is dubious if our archaeologists' work was precise enough to determine a one or two-year difference in stratigraphy regarding these. North also subjected De Vaux's pottery typology to severe criticism. Cf. as well Cross' testimony in "Scripts", p. 190, n. 9, on how he wavered back and forth between De Vaux and Milik on the matter of the bowl graffiti (related to the problem of the wall and broken dishes), finally dutifully following the former against his original judgement.

[18] See De Vaux, pp. 41ff., 66ff., and 123, recapitulated in E. M. Laperrousaz, *Qoumrân L'Établissement Essénien des bords de La Mer Morte*, Paris, 1976, pp. 61f.

[19] For evidence of habitation in some forty caves, see De Vaux, pp. 44ff., 50ff., 56ff., and 107. Cross agrees, p. 64, n. 20. There is even evidence of habitation in mere crevices or "depressions" in the cliff walls, and on p. 107, De Vaux admits that pottery types also appear to be of later date than the outside limits he himself set for the life of the community; see also Laperrousaz, p. 91 for the pottery found in these caves.

[20] Even Cross admits that the finding of an all-important commentary like Habakkuk so neatly placed in a jar along with other similar materials in Cave I implies that it was actually in use at the time of the fall of the monastery and, therefore, comprised part of the current literature of the sect. Both the evidence of some habitation and the careful appearance of the deposits in Cave I, despite some breakage, contrasts markedly with the disorder and completely disrupted state of Cave IV, where it is obvious that people of

event, after the fall of Jerusalem Jewish coins would no longer have been
considered legal tender and no one would have been using anything but
pagan coins.[21]

It is just as likely that the Romans, in destroying the settlement, simply
burned the buildings and then proceeded on to their siege of Jerusalem.[22]
Though coin evidence indicates habitation after 68 C.E., it is impossible
to say who inhabited the site from 68-73 C.E. *Inhabited caves* (as opposed
to book repositories like Cave IV) show no evidence of having been
disturbed by the Romans. Though habitation at Qumran seems to have
come to an end sometime in the seventies or eighties, evidence of not insubstantial habitation does continue at Ein Feshka, and this cannot really
be separated from Qumran.[23] For our purposes, where issues of this kind

---

hostile intent did disturb the manuscripts. Since Cave IV is located in such close proximity to the settlement, it is not surprising that it should have been disturbed at the time of the
investment of the actual settlement; however it is certainly more likely that such disturbance occurred in 136 rather than in 70 C.E. In view of the sheer magnitude of the
materials found there, it is not surprising that some have taken it for a "library" (see
Cross, p. 25, n. 29); on the other hand, if the helter-skelter disorder of the cave
characterized its state before the fall of the community, then, aside from the evidence of
deliberate mutilation, it would not be surprising if the cave was already being used as "a
genizah" before the fall of the community.

[21] Cf. De Vaux in *RB*, 60, 61, and 63, 1953, 1954, and 1956, pp. 93ff., 229ff., and
565ff.; in *Archaeology*, pp. 18ff., 33ff., 64ff., and 70f.; also Laperrousaz, pp. 30, 85, and
90.

[22] Groups could easily have filtered back to the site in the ruined conditions engendered
by war or for that matter continued living in the caves up until the time serious operations
got under way against Masada in 72-73 C.E. In this terrain pursuit was almost futile, as
the higher up the cave-punctuated cliff-face the pursuit progressed, the higher any party
could also retreat to escape—even as high as the Bethlehem plain itself. As long as any
stragglers, refugees, or hold-outs remained quiescent at Qumran and refrained from
harassing the Jericho Road (the importance of which Cross, p. 75ff., has rightly pointed
out), the Romans probably would not have bothered them to any extent. To use for the
purposes of illustration a parallel example, even the Masada sectaries do not appear to
have taken a very active role in the final stages of the uprising after their leader
Menachem was killed (*War* 2.17.8.). For these purposes, their mass suicide does not in-
dicate a particularly aggressive resistance.

We have already noted the flight of the early "Christians" from Jerusalem in this
period in response to a mysterious "oracle" not unlike those familiar to us in Qumran
scriptural exegesis. The resemblance of traditions regarding this "Pella flight of the
Jerusalem Church" to the Masada flight of "the *Sicarii*" is strong. Even the stonings of
their respective leaders, which trigger the two events, are to a certain extent parallel. Between the years 100 B.C.E. to 100 C.E., the only stoning Josephus records, aside from
those of James and his rain-making predecessor "Onias the Just", is that of this
Menachem the son or grandson of "Judas the Galilean". Josephus' pejorative "*Sicarii*"
need not be taken too seriously, because certainly the sectaries did not refer to themselves
by any such nomenclature. For their suicide as presaged by earlier ones in 37 B.C.E. and
2 and 4 Macc, as well as New Testament parodies of it, see above n. 15.

[23] That this habitation was Jewish and not Roman cannot be doubted. That non-
Jewish coins may have been found here is not particularly relevant, since, as we have
already noted, until the Bar Kochba period nothing but non-Jewish coins would have

and the cessation of habitation at Qumran generally are concerned, it is sufficient to prove that there is nothing in the available evidence that can be said with certainty, and which, therefore, warrants discarding otherwise credible *textual* theories.

Even as things presently stand, a not insubstantial number of coins from the third year of the Jewish Revolt, 68-69, have already been found at Qumran and more at Ein Feshka, and it is suprising that after the encirclement of Jerusalem as many coins as this escaped.[24] De Vaux claims that there was sufficient time between April (his presumed, but by no means proven, date for the beginning of minting) and June (the date he contends *Jewish* habitation at Qumran came to an abrupt end) for such a large number of Jewish coins to have made an appearance at Qumran. But we are well into the year 68-69 as it is. There is also a substantial number of coins too oxidized to read, and as long as these exist, doubt must persist.[25] All such matters must be carefully examined when attempting to say anything on the basis of *coin data* regarding habitational *termini* at Qumran.

Neither has a satisfactory explanation yet been given for Pliny's contention that there was an "Essene" settlement "above Ein Gedi" (in such a context, "above" probably means "north of") when he was writing after the fall of Jerusalem. Though this might be the anachronism

---

been in circulation. As against this point, see De Vaux's critique of the hypotheses of Driver and Roth in *NTS*, xiii, 1966-67, p. 102 about a "hoard" of later coins found in the Jericho area. This hoard consisted of five silver shekels from the Year 4 of the Revolt, but the exception proves the rule, and it was just this, a hoard.

[24] Though rare coins from the year 70 C.E. were also found at Masada, as in the case of the Jericho hoard above, these coins were probably the product of the final flight to Masada after the fall of Jerusalem across the Bethlehem plain past Herodion; cf. Y. Yadin, *Masada: Herod's Fortress and the Zealots' Last Stand*, London, 1966, pp. 108f. and 170f. and De Vaux in *NTS* above, pp. 102f. and 126. If commentators are correct in claiming *the buildings* at Qumran had already been destroyed (its caves being indestructible), the refugees probably would have preferred (as well as in the circumstances found it easier) to flee to Masada.

[25] De Vaux argues that after 68-69 C.E., no further *Jewish* coins were found at the site until the Bar Kochba period. But no coins have yet been found, for instance, from the Fourth Year of the Revolt on the Temple Mount (cf. B. Mazar, "The Archaeological Excavations near the Temple Mount", *Jerusalem Revealed: Archaeology in the Holy City 1968-1974*, ed. Y. Yadin, Jerusalem, 1976, p. 32). Are we to assume that the Temple then fell in 69 and not 70 C.E.? Likewise, no coins have yet been found from the First Year of the Revolt at Qumran. Does this mean that the sectaries were, therefore, absent at this time? These are, to be sure, nonsense questions, but they illustrate the kind of logic being applied and the kind of precision claimed by archaeologists at Qumran on these and similar issues. Suppose De Vaux had missed a single coin or gone on to dig a little further? With regard to the existence or non-existence of Roman arrowheads outside the settlement, he responds, "Was I supposed to dig up the whole hillside?"; *NTS*, p. 101. Where *precision* in matters as tenuous as coin data is at issue, I for one would be tempted to reply in the affirmative.

many scholars take it for, it cannot simply be dismissed as misinformed or tendentious without some explanation.[26] Certainly James' successor and reputed "cousin", the "Rechabite Priest" Simeon bar Cleophas, must have subsisted somewhere outside of Jerusalem with his community until his execution under Trajan (and by this, one does not mean at "Pella"). Where questions such as these are concerned, it must be concluded that after the period so meticulously documented by Josephus, our sources are just too sketchy to say anything with precision about the continuation or absence of habitation at Qumran or its environs. What can be agreed upon is that the site was at some point inhabited by partisans of Bar Kochba before they retreated further into the Wadi Murabba'at or the Nahal Hever after the collapse of their uprising. Any fair-minded observer has to acknowledge this as the *absolute terminus ad quem* for both *the cessation of habitation* at Qumran and the deposit of the scrolls in the caves.[27]

If the scrolls were deposited before this time, additional questions emerge. Why were they left relatively undisturbed during the period when we know that the site was occupied, not only by Romans, but also by Bar Kochba's partisans? How can one account for the fact that they, not to mention the jars, etc. (which even materially were surely not without value), were not disturbed even more than they were during these various occupations leading up to the final abandonment of the site? How are we to account for the fact that a cave like Cave I shows no signs of disturbance at all during this period? Is it conceivable that no curious inhabitants ever went up to inspect a location like Cave I, particularly when the whole area appears to have been used as a defensive perimeter of some kind by Bar Kochba's men (cf. the reference to the "*mezad ha-Hassidin*" or "the fortress of the Hassidaeans" in Bar Kochba's correspondence[28])? Certainly there is evidence of disorder and destruction in Cave IV (a cave that could not have been missed by anyone living in the "ruins" of Qumran), but how are we to account for

---

[26] *Hist Nat* 5.17.4. Pliny is most insistent here, but De Vaux, pp. 134ff. and Cross, pp. 15 and 70ff., while willing to make use of this testimony to support their identifications of the sect as "Essenes", dismiss his chronology. Cf. the hint of such a settlement in Mur 45.6 below.

[27] For the Nahal Hever finds, see Y. Aharoni, "Expedition B—The Cave of Horror"; Y. Yadin, "Expedition D"; and "Expedition D—The Cave of Letters", *Israel Exploration Journal*, 12, 1962, pp. 186-99; 11, 1961, pp. 36-52; and 12, 1962, pp. 227-57. Here, too, the evidence shows that Bar Kochba's people occupied the site. They probably abandoned it in the face of superior force, but they could not have remained unaware of Cave IV.

[28] Cf. in *DJD*,ii.xlv.6. The phrase, as it is used here, is a geographical place-name, which in all probability refers to Qumran or some place very much like it. The reference implies habitation at the site, and in the process ties groups from Judas Maccabee's "*Hassidim*" to Bar Kochba's partisans to the locale.

the fact that it was not disturbed even more than it was and why were the materials it contained simply left as they were between 68 and 136 C.E.?[29]

Regardless of how all these numerous questions will finally be answered, and satisfactory solutions will certainly never be found to all of them, 68 C.E. is nothing but *the earliest* possible date for the *deposit* of the scrolls in the caves, not the latest. There is *absolutely no finality* on these matters, not even a presumption of one. In particular, as we have already stressed, such results cannot be used to rule out theories intrinsically better than the methodologies upon which they are themselves predicated. This is particularly true when the detailed theory we have presented can fully account for almost the whole of the historical *sitz-im-leben* of, as well as almost every allusion and turn-of-phrase in, the Habakkuk *Pesher* (and as a consequence, of most of the other *pesharim* at Qumran); and where contrariwise opposing theories are hardly even able to render such data sensible. In this case, *meaningful textual analysis* which can make *real* sense out of *internal data* must take precedence over the kind of archaeological and palaeographic evidence which exists at Qumran. Problems centering about this palaeographical evidence, where there is hardly an absolute ''peg'' except the Queen Helen lapidary work (which says little about manuscripts)[30] and the Bar Kochba documents, are based on many of the same archaeological and historical preconceptions we have already discussed above.[31] But where the specific problem of the Habakkuk *Pesher*

---

[29] See our remarks concerning these caves in nn. 19-20 above.

[30] Though Cross claims ''a series of absolute dating'' pegs ''at intervals throughout the Herodian Age'' (by which he means Birnbaum's ''ossuaries'', including those of Uzziah, at Beit Schur, Ein Roghel, and Wadi Sali‘a, which the latter treats as a *single* ''peg'' even though ''the Herodian period'' endures by their definition approximately 125 years); the only really secure ''peg'' he has is Queen Helen's funerary monument which we would date in the fifties or sixties C.E. He and Avigad exhibit substantial differences over the Dominus Flevit ossuaries. Where the Beni Hezir inscription is concerned, he (''Scripts'', pp. 174, 198, and 199; in ''Oldest Manuscripts'' he confidently termed it *''a terminus ad quem''* for first century B.C.E. scripts) and Albright (''A Biblical Fragment from the Maccabean Age: the Nash Papyrus'', *SBL*, 56, 1937, p. 159) agree on a date of about the beginning of the Christian era. However, the names of the priests on the plaque and the unfinished condition of the monument (as well as that of adjoining ones) can as well relate to ''the sons of Kanthera'' in the fifties and sixties C.E. as to those ''Boethusians'' at the end of the first century B.C.E. The last of these former, Joseph Cabi, was very much connected with events relating to the death of James whose name tradition also attaches to this monument. Certainly this plaque cannot be considered a secure *terminus ad quem*, at least *not a precise one*, for first century B.C. scripts.

[31] See pp. 12ff. above. Almost all palaeographers uncritically accept De Vaux's ''earthquake'' hypothesis using it as a *terminus* to date the end of period I of Qumran habitation (cf. Birnbaum, pp. 127ff. and 149, and Cross, ''Scripts'', pp. 133ff., 173, and 199, and ''Oldest Manuscripts'', pp. 147f.). This, in itself, does not overly distort the chronology since the proper *terminus* (if there was a total abandonment at Qumran and not simply a diminution in habitation) is Herod's final assumption of power in Palestine in 37 B.C.E.;

is the issue, palaeographic evidence, as we have noted, is not a significant factor. Where relevant to the Qumran corpus as a whole, I have treated it in detail elsewhere.[32]

---

but almost all, as well, uncritically accept his determination of 68 C.E. for the cessation of *Jewish* habitation in the region of Qumran, and, therefore, for the deposit of the scrolls in the caves—a precarious thesis at best. In addition, most of the usual historical and sociological assumptions behind such determinations are the warp and woof of their general textual and historical approach.

[32] *Maccabees, Zadokites, Christians and Qumran*, pp. 28-32 and 78-91.

APPENDIX

THE "THREE NETS OF BELIAL"
IN THE ZADOKITE DOCUMENT AND
"*BALLA^c*"/"BELA^c" IN THE TEMPLE SCROLL

Directly upon its exegesis of Ez 44:15, the Zadokite Document raises the "three nets of Belial" charge against the Jerusalem establishment. These, it contends, were erected by "Belial" as "three kinds of Righteousness" in order to ensare Israel. It enumerates these as "*Zanut*" (fornication), "*Hon*" (Riches), and "*teme⁵ ha-Mikdash*" (pollution of the Sanctuary). While one or another of these charges could relate to any establishment in any time or place, taken together, they concretize the general thrust of the critique as anti-Herodian ("Belial" in such a context has interesting connotations where Josephus' description of the new practices introduced by Herod are concerned, and one should also note its relation to the "*balla^c*"/"Bela^c" esotericisms below and the language of "*leval^co*"/"*leval^cam*" we have already delineated).

Though usually taken as directed against the Jerusalem priesthood, priests are nowhere mentioned as such. Rather these accusations are accompanied by ongoing evocation of a Pauline-type adversary, who is referred to as a "windbag"/"spouter" and connected from CD,iv to viii with allusions to Lying prophets crying "peace when there is no peace" (Ez 13:10ff.; *n.b.*, Josephus' "Saulus" is the intermediary between "all those desirous of peace" and Agrippa II), a "blaspheming Tongue", "pouring out Lies", "daubing upon the wall", "departing from the Way" (in CD,i-ii, "leading astray in a trackless waste without a Way" and "removing the boundary markers"; *n.b.*, the inversion here of "wilderness"/"Way" imageries), and "the Way of Traitors."

The "Riches" charge, which recurs throughout these sections, is usually accompanied by the imagery of "fornication". It carries the general meaning of the Habakkuk *Pesher*'s "robbing the Poor", "gathering Riches", and "profiteering from the spoils of the peoples", and even includes an allusion to separation from "the uncleanness of the Temple treasure" (CD,vi.16). The allusion to "peoples" both here and in the Zadokite Document concretizes the kind of "profiteering" (CD,viii.7) being envisioned, linking it directly to Herodians and violent Gentiles generally.

The fornication charge, however, is crucial for determining the historical provenance of the critique. It is explained in terms of taking a second wife while the first is still living, in support of which "two by two" and "male and female" quotations from Genesis are invoked. Where the Ruler is concerned, it is treated here and in the Temple Scroll as a variation of the Deuteronomic "not multiplying wives unto himself" and clearly involves *both* polygamy and divorce. The Temple Scroll makes the "divorce" aspect to the charge concrete and generalizes it further at the end in lxvi.8ff. where the seduction of a virgin is at issue and the ban on marrying nieces is enunciated. It is safe to say that, though Rabbinic Judaism in theory permitted polygamy and divorce, these practices were nevertheless rare. More importantly, there is no indication whatsoever that

Maccabeans indulged in either to any extent. The opposite can be said of Herodians.

Consonant with its length and greater systematization, the Temple Scroll also goes into more detail than the Zadokite Document concerning the Deuteronomic King Law, adding the all-important stricture, *"thou shall not put a foreigner over you"* (italics mine; Deut 17:15ff.). There is no doubt that the recommendation against foreign kings has little relevance to any period except the Herodian; not even the Seleucid or Persian—certainly not the Maccabean. Had it not been specifically evoked in 11QT,lvi.15, we would have had to postulate it. Also where the King is concerned, the Temple Scroll further develops the Zadokite Document's not taking another wife during the lifetime of the first and "not multiplying wives" to include not taking a wife except from among Israelites and taking one wife, and one wife only during her lifetime and *never divorcing* (11QT,lvii.17f.). These recitations are so forced as to make their purpose almost certain, and their anti-Herodian flow, both as regards Herodian kings and Herodian princesses (cf. CD,v.10), should be clear. More narrowly, they are always directed against persons connected in some way with the families of Agrippa I and Agrippa II who indulged in these practices promiscuously and as a matter of course. To be much plainer Qumran would have had literally *to name* its respondents.

We have already noted the "pollution of the Sanctuary" charge in the Habakkuk *Pesher*, where together with the theme of "Abominations" (as per the imagery of Ez 44:6ff., where it is directed against the admission of those "uncircumcised either in heart or body" into the Temple), it is directed against the disqualification in Zadokite terms of the Wicked Priest ("who did not circumcize the foreskin of his heart"). In 11QT,lxvi.14f. the Habakkuk *Pesher*'s "Abominations"/"*To^cevot*" is linked to the two matters of divorce and marrying nieces and elsewhere, to other matters involving Gentiles. For its part, the Zadokite Document, following upon its discussion of "fornication", "Riches", and the Deuteronomic King Law, introduces the theme of "separation", *i.e.*, "separation from impure things", to explain this charge of Temple pollution. The "separation" referred to is the sort described in 11QT,xlvi.10 and at the root of the Temple wall incident directed against Agrippa II, *i.e.*, the separation of the Temple from the city and the separation from the Temple of unclean groups like lepers, menstruating women, etc. (including Herodians, as the concrete charge of "sleeping with women during their periods" in CD,v.7 and the curious play on the word *"balla^c"* in the Temple Scroll will make plain), not only from the Temple, but also the area around the Temple.

This theme of "pollution of the Sanctuary" permeates the fabric of the Temple Scroll (cf. particularly 11QT,xlv-lii), when it comes to the separation of impure persons from the Temple and separating the Temple from the city (11QT,xlv-vi—matters echoed in CD,vi.12ff.'s barring the door of the Temple and separating from "the sons of the Pit...and polluted Riches"; cf. Acts 21:28ff. on Paul's disbarment from the Temple including both the notes about "polluting the Temple" and "barring the door"). Where the theme of "separation" in the Zadokite Document is concerned, the relationship of such allusions to *Herodians* is made explicit. Some translators actually place a "because" between the charge of "polluting the Temple" and "sleeping with women in their periods", but there is no "because" in the text, only the conjunction "and"—the first being the general charge; the second, only one of its several aspects. The guilt of the Jerusalem priesthood, as is made clear in CD,v.14f., is guilt by association. The priests have polluted the Temple by associating with and accepting gifts or sacrifices from such classes of persons, *i.e.*, "Rich" Herodians and other foreigners or people in touch with such persons (the problem of the pollution of the Temple treasure). The text is not saying that Ananus or other priests "slept with women during their periods" (anymore than it is in the next sentence that *they married their nieces*), only that by associating in various ways with people who did, they brought upon themselves and the Temple the general pollution.

Of course, one can be fairly confident that no Jewish priesthood, whatever corruptions or pollutions imputed to it, Maccabean, Sadducean, Boethusian, or some other, ever indulged in "sleeping with women in their periods", and no accusation of such is on record—most certainly not where Maccabeans are concerned (nor is there any record in regard to them of undue divorce, marriage with nieces, or Riches). The sexual behaviour of Agrippa I and Agrippa II cannot be determined with any precision from the material available to us, though both were brought up in Rome and both would have been seen as guilty by association. One can be fairly certain, however, that neither Titus nor the infamous Felix observed Jewish scrupulousness over sexual relations during a woman's menstrual flow. For Qumran this charge precisely reflects how Agrippa I, Agrippa II, Herodias, Bernice, Drusilla, and others, with their easy-going Hellenized ways, would have been seen. In this regard, too, one should not forget the rumor conserved by Josephus of Bernice's fornication with her brother Agrippa (a charge echoed very specifically in CD,viii.6f. where the "whorish ways and sinful Riches" of "the princes of Judah" were at issue—in viii.10 "the Kings of the peoples"/"*amim*," in this context very definitely alluding to Herodians). One can be fairly confident, too, that these condemnations were part and parcel of the reasons why *Agrippa II and Bernice* were ultimately barred from Jerusalem by "the Innovators" and their palaces burned.

That this fornication during menstruation charge was directed against Herodians is verified in the next sentence, where the specific claim is raised, that "each man marries the daughter of his brother or sister." It is clear from the phraseology of the latter that we have to do with *frequency of occurrence* and *habituality*. To be sure there are examples in the Talmud of marriage with nieces, but as with polygamy, these are noteworthy rather for the testimony they provide of the infrequency of the practice. As with polygamy and divorce, there is *no evidence* that the Maccabees indulged in the practice to any extent, if at all. Only *one group, and one group only*, can be said to have done this *habitually* or as *a matter of course*—Herodians. They married their nieces and close cousins *regularly* as a matter of seeming family policy. When persons who did, in fact, pollute themselves in such a manner entered the Temple and were not properly "separated" from it (the essence of the improper "separation" charge), then, of course, a general pollution ensued.

The references to a "Tongue full of insults" and the "Abominations of the vipers" run on until the treatment of the "serpents" and the condemnation of "the windbag and the Lying Spouter's spouting" in CD,viii.13. One should note that at this point the Zadokite Document is speaking in terms of the "New Covenant", language which links up in this period absolutely with Josephus' discussions of "Innovators"/"innovations" and problems relating to accepting gifts and sacrifices from or on behalf of foreigners in the Temple, as well as the admission into the precincts of the Temple of persons "uncircumcized in heart or body" as per the vocabulary of Ez 44:7 and 1QpHab,xi.13—"the New Covenant" or "innovations" having to do with envisioning precisely the opposite set of circumstances. All of these matters are concretized in some detail in the Temple Scroll, as we have seen, including the ban on marriage with a niece, divorce, foreign kings, the demand for proper "separation", etc. In turn, they are systematically *inverted* in the New Testament with its *retrospective* portrait of the "Hellenized" Christ *preferring* the company of just such classes of persons, *i.e.*, "Sinners", "prostitutes", "tax-collectors", people not observing Jewish dietary regulations, etc. This portrait of Christ "eating" with "Sinners", "fornicators", etc., has particular relevance within the ideological framework of the presentation of Jesus as "Temple" elsewhere in the New Testament and Eph 2:11ff.'s insistence on there being no "aliens" or "visiting foreigners".

With regard to innovations of the opposite kind, *i.e.* those "set up by Belial as three kinds of Righteousness" in CD,iv.12ff. above and Herod in *Ant.* 15.10.4, the language of 11QT,xlvif. on "separating" unclean classes of persons from the Temple (the essence of the Temple wall affair involving Agrippa II above and the related incident directed by "Simon" against his father Agrippa I) concentrates the focus of all these matters on a single issue. Pursuant to a notice about "the children of Israel ... entering my Temple" (7f.) and playing on the language of "swallowing" so characteristic of attacks at Qumran on the Herodian establisment from Belial in CD,iv to *leval^{c}o/leval^{c}am/teval^{c}enu* in 1QpHab,viii-ix; it reads: "Make a barrier around the Temple one hundred cubits wide (high?) in order *to separate* the Holy Temple from the city and *should not come* (plural) *balla^c/Bela^c* into My Temple, *nor violate* it" (plural; italics mine). The passage varies Nu 4:20's "*che-valla^c*" dropping the "*che*" and Job 20:15's "*hayil bala^c*". "swallowing Riches." In its second part it employs the "pollution"/"violation of the Temple" vocabulary of Lv 21:12, Ez 22:26, 22:39, and most importantly Ez 44:7. It closes with an imprecation which plays on "seeing" from Nu 4:20 (the actual point of conflict in the Agrippa II affair) to produce "fearing", itself having interesting repercussions vis-a-vis "God-fearers" (though the citation could be read, "nor see into My sanctuary", not "fearing"). Although "*bala^c*" might simply be obscure here, what appears to have been reproduced in this passage is "Bela^c", not *balla^c*.

Whether these things are deliberate or not is difficult to determine, as is the meaning of "*heil*" in the above context (whether a barrier or high wall of some kind, or a Job 20:15-like esotericism); but in view of the evocation of the name of the father of both Bela^c and Balaam, "Be^{c}or", in the constant reiteration in the next column of "in skins sacrificed to idols", bearing on the issue of gifts and/or other offerings to the Temple (probably either Gentile or Herodian) and the association of the parallel "pollution of the Temple with idols" and eating "food sacrificed to idols" with "Beliar"/"Balaam" in 2 Co 6 and Rev 2:14 below, in our view it *is* purposeful. We have discussed the correspondence of these "pollution of the Temple"/"pollution of the body"/"Christ" and "Beliar" materials above, pp. 19f.

"Bela^c" is the name of the first Edomite king in the Old Testament (Cf. Ge 14:ff.—the five kings of the plain, Ge 35:31, 36:32f., and 1 Ch 1:43f.). His father is "Be^{c}or", making the name indistinguishable from its variation "Balaam the son of Be^{c}or" (cf. the evocation of the latter in 2 Pe 2:15 below). A second "Bela^c" is the firstborn son of *Benjamin* in Ge 46:21, Nu 26 and 1 Ch 7-8, which sets up interesting resonances with Paul's claim to be of "the tribe of Benjamin." For Ju 19-20 "the sons of Belial" are also Benjaminites, inhabitants of Saul's Gibeah, and their reprehensible *sexual* acts make their name a byword (for 2 Sam 16:7, 20:1, and 2 Ch 13:7, the usage is often applied to Benjaminites in close association with "Saul" opposing the Davidic king line in some manner; and for 1 Ki 21:13, two "sons of Belial" are directly involved—at the instigation of *Jezebel*—in *the stoning* of Naboth for *blasphemy* and *opposing the King*).

Seen in these senses, it is possible to read the letters *B-L-ᶜ* as a *circumlocution for Herodians* (an identification already independently arrived at in relation to the "Belial" usage in the Zadokite Document when considering euphemisms like "sleeping with women in their periods" and "marrying nieces"). That "Belaᶜ" (the name of an Edomite king and "Balaam" interchangeable with it) is intended as a circumlocution for *Herodians* is reinforced by the *plural* usages that accompany it throughout the citation. If this is true, then not only, therefore, would the "Belaᶜ" esotericism be a variation of the "Belial" terminology, but it provides further confirmation of the historical provenance of these matters as relating integrally to the exclusion of Herodians and other foreigners from the Temple in the middle of the first century C.E., as we have developed it from our analysis in a third independent textual context, that of the Habakkuk *Pesher* (cf. too the same set of allusions relating to "the sons of Belial" in 1QH,iv.10ff., including "Scoffers of Deceit"/"Scoffers of Lying", "Tongue", "lips", etc. *N.b.*, the common vocabularly it shares with 4QpNah,ii and 2 Pe/Jude below. 1QH,iv even hints at the relationship of these "sons of Belial"/Herodians to the "*conspiracy*"—"*zamam*"/"*zammu*"—of the Wicked Priest to remove the Righteous Teacher, not surprisingly also containing the foregoing intimations which in our view hint at the role of a genre of persons like Josephus' "Saulus" or the New Testament's "Saul" as part and parcel of these events). Yet another confirmation of the correctness of the historical provenance we have specified for these materials is 11QT,xlvi.11's use of "*yehalluhu*", which cannot be divorced from the central role this same usage plays (amid the language of "Covenant-breaking", "*Toᶜevot*", "the sons of Zadok", etc.) in Ez 44:7ff.'s ban on "bringing strangers uncircumcised in heart or flesh into My Temple *to pollute it*" (italics mine).

In particular Job 20:15 above could not have helped appealing to the sectaries, referring as it does to "swallowing Riches", "stealing from the Poor", the "Tongue", and "the poison of asps"; cf. CD,viii.19ff. relating this last usage to "the Kings of the peoples" (*i.e.*, Herodians) and ultimately "Gehazi", a favorite circumlocution in Rabbinic literature for persons connected with early Christianity like Paul. This "Gehazi" allusion is invoked in CD,viii.21 in relation to "preaching wind and the Lying Spouter's spouting" and "rejecting the commandments of God and abandoning them in stubbornness of heart" (the subject of these last, "the builders of"/"daubers upon the wall", relates to Ez 13:10ff. where it has the specific sense of "Lying prophets" crying "peace when there is no peace"; cf. that "Saulus" above who is the intermediary between "all those desirous of peace" in Jerusalem and Agrippa II outside it—the 'peace alliance' ultimately inviting the Romans into the city to suppress the Revolt). The "Gehazi" reference is followed in CD,viii by allusion to "betraying the New Covenant in the land of Damascus" and the material about the "standing up of the Messiah of Aaron and Israel," which we have already interpreted in terms of a Messianic "return".

Balaam and Gehazi were two of four commoners Rabbinic literature repeatedly insists would have no share in the world to come and no portion among the Righteous. Directly upon its play on "Balaam" as "swallower of the people" and "Be^cor" as "*be^cir*," *i.e.*, "animal", in 105a; b. San 106b applies Job 20:15 above to Do³eg, a third of these "enemies"/"scoffers" (cf. Do³eg the *Edomite* over Saul's bodyguard, called "Benjaminites" in 1 Sam 22, who betrays David and slaughters eighty-five priests in "linen ephods"; in particular, note Ps 52 connecting him, in the context of "swallowing" imagery, to the "Tongue", "doing deceit"/"*^coseh remiyyah*"—as opposed to "speaking Righteousness", "Lying"/"*Sheker*", "the deceitful Tongue loving words of swallowing"/"*bala^c*", "Riches", etc.).

B. San 106a links Balaam, Job ("the Enemy"; cf. too 1 Pe 5:8 linking "the Enemy" with "swallowing"), and Jethro (the latter being further linked to Cain and Kenites); and 109bf. takes up Korah, another of those who "will have no share in the world to come," who contended with Moses. Jude 11 specifically evokes three of these Adversaries, Cain, Balaam, and Korah in the same verse. The Letter of Jude is replete with the Qumran-style language of "fornication", "darkness", "pollution", a person with "a mouth full of boasts", "the Day of Judgement" (cf. 1QpHab,xii.14-xiii.2), "fire" (x.5), rain imagery, "the Lord coming with his myriads of Holy Ones" (1QM,xif.), and "murmurers, complainers walking in their own lusts ... for the sake of gain" (cf. 1QH,iv.7-22 on "the sons of Belial" and 1QpHab,v.7f). Even more strikingly, Jude 10, introducing these allusions to "the way of Cain, profiteering from the error of Balaam, and perishing (*i.e.*, "being swallowed") in the contentiousness of Korah", makes pointed reference to "*animals*", which in this context can only be seen as a play on the name of "Be^cor" in the manner of that of b. San 105a above.

Preceding its evocation of this *be^cir*/"animal" theme, b. San 105a further identifies Be^cor with "Cushan-Rishathaim and Laban." In Ju 3:4ff., the former is related to having a Gentile king put over the Israelites because of fornication and intermarriage with foreigners. In Ge 31:23f., the latter relates to how Laban "pursued after" ("*radaph aharei*") *Jacob*. This last phrase is, in turn, identical with and probably at the root of the language employed by 1QpHab,xi.6 (itself culminating in "swallowing" imagery) to describe the destruction of the Righteous Teacher, *i.e.*, "the Wicked Priest pursued after the Righteous Teacher to swallow" or "destroy him"—or varying the allusion slightly, "to *Bela^c* him", that is to say, to do the things the Herodian establishment characteristically did, "consume the people". As in Is 2:5 preceding Is 3:10, the further resonance of "Jacob" with the name James provides an additional correspondence should one choose to regard it (cf. too CD,i.21's use of "*yirddephu*" to describe the assault by "the Lying Scoffer", "the Seekers after Smooth Things", and those "breaking the Law"—*yapheiru-hok*—on "the Righteous One", which we would identify with an earlier assault on James, the one by Paul described in Pseudoclementine tradition, refracted to a certain extent in Acts; cf. too the parallel note of violent pursuit in both traditions).

No less important in continuation of this theme of avoiding "pollution of the Sanctuary" and having regard to the "separation" of "clean" and "unclean" things in the Temple (a dichotomy alluded to esoterically by Paul in exposition of James' directives to overseas communities in 2 Co 6:14ff.), 11QT,xlvii.13ff. specifically raises the issue of "food" or "things sacrificed to idols". This is always attached to the Hebrew "*beᶜorot*", which literally means "in skins", producing a solecisim, *i.e.*, one cannot speak of "skins sacrificed to idols", only "beasts" or "animals" (a secondary root meaning of *B-ᶜ-R, yod* and *waw* being generally interchangeable in Qumran epigraphy; cf. too "things immolated to idols" in the Koranic redaction below, also related to this root).

Since unclean vessels were considered to render the foodstuffs within them unclean, not to mention their bearers (cf. b. Hull 129a), it is proper to ask, who was bringing such "skins" into the Temple and from where? Since, in addition, skins were considered to lead to the spoilage of grain (b. Pes 45b) and were hardly a fit vehicle for oil, this would leave them as useful containers only for water and perhaps wine. The point about skins, however, was that *they were valuable* (being used for such things as parchment, aprons, shoes, cushions, bed coverings, rugs, etc.) and that *the high priests were allowed to keep them* (M. Shek 6:6). Xlvii's exaggerated concern over "skins", then, can be seen as an aspect of its more general one over Gentile gifts in the Temple and the consumption of "things sacrificed to idols" (and idolatry in general), and the "pollution" connected to both (cf. James' Acts 15:20 proscription on "the pollutions of the idols ...", which, in fact, would include this narrower proscription on "skins sacrificed to idols"). In this context, a reference to "polluted" offerings of some kind entering the Temple (or for that matter the body) most likely relates to the kinds of things that were being said about Herodians and those priests or "Violent Ones" associated with them.

However these things may be, it is the "pollutions of"/"things sacrificed to idols", which produced the resonances that so interested the community especially where gifts from overseas were concerned. The category of "food"/ "things sacrificed to idols," as should be clear, is a *key element* in *James' directives* to overseas communities, as conserved for us in Acts 15:29 and 21:25 and reflected in 1 Co 8:1ff., 10:19ff., 2 Co 6:16 (*n.b.* the specific reference to "Belial" and "light" and "dark" imagery here), and Re 2:14ff. (*n.b.* here the attribution of the license to consume such "food" to Balaam and the reiteration of the typical "nets" and "fornication" themes, *i.e.*, he "taught Balak *to cast a snare before the sons of Israel, to eat things sacrificed to idols and commit fornication*"; italics mine. Cf. too the parallel accusation in 2 Pe 2:15 that "Balaam", described as "loving Unrighteousness", led Israel "astray from the Right Way", surrounded by the intense imagery of "fornication", "pollutions", "licentiousness", "Darkness", "Day of Judgement"/"end of days", "scoffing", and echoed in Jude 11 above amid the kindred imagery of "murmuring", "walking in their own lusts", "scoffers in the last times", "greed", and "Judgement" executed by God's Elect).

Not only is James' ban on 'food sacrificed to idols', which appears in few other known contexts, a common concern of all these documents (*n.b.*, its reappearance accompanied by allusion to "blood", "carrion", and "strangled animals" in Muhammad's instructions to a more recent *ummah* in Ko 2:172, 5:3, 16:115, etc.); it takes on new meaning in the context of the allusions signalled above in the Temple Scroll and what one can surmise to have been the behavior of Herodians and their consorts in regard to it, particularly those from "Asia"—not to mention that of other "*nilvim*"/"*ᶜamim*"/"*ᶜArizei-Goʾim*". In this regard the evocation of the Jamesian position on this issue in an *Asian* context in Re 2:14ff. is particularly revealing. The evocation of a variation of this proscription in the Temple Scroll ties concerns evinced in it directly to concerns associated by tradition with the *historical James*. That both "Be'or", the father at once of both Bela' and Balaam, and "Do'eg" are Edomite names provides further scope for known Qumran predilection for word-play and sets up additional interesting resonances with the Bela'/Balaam/Belial equivalence above.

The usage "pollute"/"violate" in 11QT,xlvi.11 above provides additional insight too into our decipherment of "the Judgements of Evil" material tied to the "vengeance taken upon the corpse of the Wicked Priest" in 1QpHab,ix.1ff. (cf. the parallel allusion to "*kin'at Mishpatei-Zedek*" in 1QS,iv.4f.), *i.e.*, we have to do not with "illnesses", but "pollutions", *viz.*, "*they* inflicted the Judgements of Evil *by* committing the scandals of evil pollutions *on him in* taking vengeance upon the flesh of his corpse" (again the plurals "they inflicted" and "committed upon him" confirm that we have to do with something "done" *by others* "to him"—not a *disease*, *i.e.*, the brutal and outrageous violations "*they* inflicted" upon "*his corpse*"; italics mine).

GLOSSARY OF HEBREW TERMS

I have preferred simple Hebrew transliterations and, therefore, have abjured diacritical markings. Beginning *aleph*s also were not transliterated. In transliterating the Hebrew letter *tsadi*, I used "*z*", despite confusions in transliterating *zayin*, in order to conserve the common spelling of expressions like *Zaddik*, Zadok, Nazoraean, etc. (there are several *tsadi*s, but few *zayin*s). I preferred the double "*s*" in *Hassidim*.

abeit-galuto, a defective expression in 1QpHab,xi.6 connected with the arrest/destruction of the Righteous Teacher. While obscure and usually translated "House of his Exile", it most likely has a different meaning altogether relating to the Wicked Priest's *judicial conspiracy to destroy* to Righteous Teacher, *i.e.*, "he pursued (after) the Righteous Teacher to destroy *him* in *his* hot anger in *his beit-galut*"—meaning, "*his beit-din*"/"*beit-mishpat*" or "*his* guilty trial" (italics mine).

Aharonim/Dor ha-Aharon, the Last/Last Generation; the opposite of *ha-Rishonim*, the First. Just as the first Covenant was associated with the *Rishonim*, the New Covenant was associated with the *Aharonim* of the Last Times; *n.b.*, how Paul refers to himself as "last" in 1 Co 15:8, a nuance not lost in N.T. parodies of the expression; cf. also *ha-kez ha-aharon* (the last end) and *aharit ha-yamim* (the last days).

ʿam/ʿamim, people/peoples. In the Habakkuk *Pesher* and Zadokite Document referring to people (primarily Gentiles) "led astray" by a guilty establishment and its "ways" (cf. CD.viii.8, 16, and 47 and 1QpHab,viii.5, 11, and ix.5). Particularly the plural has the sense of "Herodians", *i.e.*, "the Kings of the peoples" (CD,viii.10); cf. also *yeter ha-ʿamim*—"other Gentiles"—for Romans below.

ʿamal, works, *ʿamalam*, their works; equivalent to "suffering works" or "works with soteriological force" as per the usage in Is 53:11f. (where it occurs in conjunction with other familiar Qumranisms such as *Daʿat, Rabbim, nephesh, Zaddik*, etc.). In 1QpHab,viii.2 and x.12, used in relation to both "Jamesian" works and "Pauline" works, the former (with *amanatam* below) in the context of eschatological exegesis of Hab 2:4.; the latter, the "empty works" of "the Liar"/"Empty Man".

amanatam, their faith. A pregnant expression in 1QpHab,viii.2 found together with *ʿamalam* in the exegesis of Hab 2:4's "the Righteous shall live by his faith" and interpreted to mean, their faith in the Righteous Teacher; in ii.1 and ii.4 the usage *heʾeminu* ("believed"/"did not believe") is an ironic reference to the central focus of the teaching of the "Man of Lying"/"Jesting".

ʿamod/ʿomdim, stand up/standing; usually translated in Qumran texts as come/coming, but evoking Ez 37:10's "they stood up" and carrying something of the connotation of "be resurrected"; cf. precisely this use in Dn 12:13 and its reflection in Lam.R,ii.3.6. Found in the Zadokite Document both in the context of eschatological exegesis of the Zadokite Covenant and allusion to the Messianic return; for the latter, see also Lam.R, intro, xxiv, applying this usage to the "return of Moses and the Patriarchs."

ʿAni (pl. *ʿAniyyim/ʿAnavim*), also *ʿAnavei-Arez*, the Meek or Downtrodden; one of the sect's several interchangeable forms of self-designation. The equivalent of similar N.T. allusions; used synonymously with *Ebionim*, the Poor, and *Dallim*.

Anshei-(H)amas, Unruly Men or Men of Violence; a synonym of *ʿArizim/ʿArizei-Goʾim* below and most likely "the Men of War" in CD,viii.37 ("who walked with the Man of Lying"). In 1QpHab,viii.11 the allusion is to the guilty wealth which the Wicked Priest "collects" through them.

Anshei-Hesed, the Men of Piety or Pious Ones equivalent to the *Hassidim*; mistranslated as "Famous Men" in Ecclesiasticus.

Anshei Kodesh-Tamim, the Men of Perfect Holiness; equivalent to such other Qumran usages characterizing communal membership as the Men of the Perfection of Holiness (*Anshei-Tamim ha-Kodesh*), the Perfect of the Way (*Tamimei-Derech*), and the Poor Ones of Piety (*Ebionei-Hesed*); cf. "Perfection of Holiness" in 2 Co 7:1.

ʿArizim, the Violent Ones; connected in 1QpHab,ii.6 and 10f. with "the Man of Lying", and "Covenant-Breakers"; cf. the parallel New Testament expression "Men of Violence" and the *Anshei-(H)amas/ʿamim* above.

ʿArizei-Goʾim, "the Violent Ones of the Gentiles"; in 4QpPs 37,ii.20 and iv.10 they play an analogous role to Josephus' "Idumaeans" and pay back the Wicked Priest for his destruction of the Righteous Teacher.

ʿAvlah, Evil or Sinning; sometimes translated as "Lying" as in "the town of Lying" erected by the Liar in 1QpHab,x.6 or the imagery of 1QS,iv,9-17.

ʿavodah, work in the sense of "service" or "mission". To be distinguished from the more soteriological *ʿamal* above and *maʿaseh/maʿasim* below. Often used when discussing the "mission" or "service" of the Liar (cf. *ʿavodat-shavo*—worthless work; 1QpHab,x.11 and *ʿavodat-tumʾah*—work of pollution; 1QS,iv.10) and those breaking off association with him in CD,viii.30, 1QS,viii.22, and ix.8; see also *leʿovdam*, serving them (*i.e.*, serving idols) in 1QpHab,xii.14.

ballaʿ/Belaʿ, as used in the Temple Scroll, varying the language of Nu 4:20 and Job 20:15 and playing on all the "swallowing" language at Qumran from Belial to *levalʿo/levalʿam/tevalʿenu* below to produce "Belaʿ", a circumlocution for Herodians; important for linking the notice in 11QT,xlvi.10 to its historical setting—*the Temple Wall incident directed against Agrippa II*. Cf. *Belaʿ an Edomite King* in Ge 14:2ff. and 36:32f. and its variations "Belial" (CD,iv.14f. and 1QH,iv.10) and "Balaam" (Re 2:14ff., 2 Pe 2:15, and Jude—the first three all making allusion to "nets" and "snares"; the last, "food sacrificed to idols"). One should also note the further adumbration of this terminology "Benjamin" and compare it to Paul's claims of "Benjaminite" ancestry.

Beit ha-Mishpat, "House of Judgement"; in 1QpHab,viii.2 used in conjunction with *ʿamalam, amanatam*, "doing *Torah*", and "being saved" in the eschatological exegesis of Hab 2:4. X.3 concretizes it as the actual *decision* of eschatological Judgement of "fire and brimstone" which God delivers through His Elect "in the midst of many nations" on all Gentiles and Jewish backsliders; cf. *Mishpatei-Esh* in x.13, 2 Pe 2:9, Jude 15, Re 20:4ff., etc., and *Mishpat, Yom ha-Mishpat* below.

Beit-Yehudah, the House of Judah or "Jews"; as used in 1QpHab,viii.2 to be distinguished from the Ephraim usage in 4QpNah, *i.e.*, Jews, as opposed to *Gentile nilvim* misled by a Lying teacher. Together with *ʿOsei-Torah*, it restricts the soteriological efficacy of the exegesis of Hab 2:4 in a two-fold manner, *i.e.*, *only to Jews*, and of these, only to *Torah*-Doers; cf. too its use in the eschatological exegesis of Ez 44:15 in CD,iv.11.

beʿorot, "in skins" (also possibly beasts/burnt offerings); as used in 11QT,xlvii.13ff., always connected to "things" or "food sacrificed to idols", a key element in *James'* directives to overseas communities as conserved in Acts 15:29 and 21:25 (in Acts 15:20, "the pollutions of the idols") and reflected in 1 Co 8:1ff., 10:19ff., 2 Co 6:16 (*n.b.*, the specific reference to "Belial" and "light" and "dark" imagery), and Re 2:14ff. (*n.b.*, the attribution of the license to consume such "food" to "Balaam" and the allusions accompanying it to "snare" and "fornication" as in CD,iv.13ff. In regard to this last, one should note the possible play on "Beʿor", the father at once of both "Belaʿ" and "Balaam". This kind of word-play is known in b. San 105a).

bezaʿ, profiteered, as in 1QpHab,ix.5 on how "the last priests of Jerusalem profiteered from the spoils—or looting—of the peoples" (*ʿamim, i.e.*, Herodians and "Violent Gentiles" generally); cf. the same usage in CD,viii.7.

Bnei-Zadok, the sons of Zadok; usually considered to imply genealogical descent, however as used at Qumran, particularly in the Zadokite Document, incorporating a play on the meaning of the root *Z-D-K* and carrying thereby a figurative sense; equivalent to many parallel usages like "sons of Light", "sons of Truth", "sons of

Righteousness'', etc.; when used eschatologically, also equivalent to N.T. expressions like ''sons of the Resurrection''—even ''sons of God''.

Bogdim, Traitors, an important expression in the *pesharim* and the Zadokite Document, denoting those within the community who ''departed from the Way'' no longer following the Law (CD,i.12f.). In 1QpHab,ii.1ff. referred to with the Man of Lying as ''Covenant-Breakers'' and synonymous with ''the House of Absalom and those of their persuasion'' in v.8ff. These did not ''believe'' what they heard ''*in the end of days*'' from the Righteous Teacher. That these include ''Violent Gentiles'' is made clear from the ʿ*Arizei-Go'im* usage and a comparison of CD,viii.4f. with viii.16; cf. N.T. inversions/parodies.

Cohanei-Yerushalaim ha-Aharonim, in 1QpHab,ix.4f. ''the last priests of Jerusalem'' who ''profiteered from the spoil of the peoples'' and whose wealth would be given over in the last days to the army of the *Kittim*; probably reflective of first-century euphemisms like ''high priests''/''chief priests''.

Daʿat, Knowledge, a basic concept at Qumran very much connected with the terminology of Is 53:11 and the process of justification generally; in some vocabularies *Gnosis*.

Dal (pl. *Dallim*), the Poor or the Meek, related to ʿ*Ani* above and *Ebion* below.

Derech, ''the Way'', related to 1QS,viii-ix's exegesis of Is 40:3, Noahic ''Perfection'' notation, ''straightening'' allusions, and New Testament ''Way'' allusions; often inverted when ''the way of the people'', the way ''of the Kings of the peoples'', and ''the Ways of the Traitors'', ''Abominations'', ''Uncleanness'', ''fornication'', etc. are at issue.

Ebion (pl. *Ebionim*), the Poor; in 1QpHab,xii.3ff. related to the predatory activities of the Wicked Priest and his destruction of the community's leadership. Another of the sect's interchangeable forms of self-designation, as well as the name applied by the early Church to ''Jewish Christians''.

Ebionei-Hesed, the Poor Ones of Piety (1QH,v.23); another of the sect's interchangeable forms of self-designation combining, like such parallel usages as *Tamimei-Derech*, *Nimharei-Zedek*, *Anshei Kodesh-Tamim*, etc., two fundamental notations.

Emet, Truth, a basic concept at Qumran; together with *Hesed*, *Zedek*, and *Daʿat* perhaps the most basic; often used in conjunction with *Derech*, Foundation and Cornerstone imagery, and *Daʿat*. An expression like ''sons of Your Truth'' parallels formulations like ''sons of Light'', ''sons of Zadok'', ''sons of *Hesed*'', and corresponding N.T. allusions.

ʿ*ezah*/ʿ*Azat ha-Yahad*, council or Community Council, with interesting resonances with ''the Jerusalem Council''; also having the connotation of ''their approach'' or ''their persuasion'' as ʿ*azatam* in 1QpHab,v.10.

ger-nilveh, resident alien. An important allusion playing on the sense of ''joining'' or ''being attached to'' of *nilveh*. Its use in 4QpNah,ii.9 prepares the way for a clearer understanding of the exegesis of ''the Zadokite statement'' in CD,iv and elucidation of ''the *Peta'ei*-Ephraim'' in 4QpNah,iii.5f.; *see nilvu/nilvim* below.

geviot, sometimes translated ''body'', but actually ''corpse''; a pivotal usage for correctly identifying the Wicked Priest in 1QpHab,ix.1f.'s ''they inflicted the Judgements of Evil by committing on him the scandals of evil pollutions in taking vengeance on *the flesh of his corpse*'' (italics mine).

hamato, his wrath; in 1QpHab,xi.5f., the ''angry wrath'' with which ''the Wicked Priest pursued the Righteous Teacher.'' Though thought in xi.14f. to relate to his ''drunkenness'', the allusion, which plays on and inverts xi.6's imagery of ''anger'' and ''consuming'', is to that divine ''cup of wrath'' which would be ''poured out'' upon the Wicked Priest. Cf. Re 14:9f. in precisely this vein: ''He shall drink the wine of God's wrath poured unmixed into the cup of his anger, and he shall be tormented in fire and brimstone...'' For the latter image see 1QpHab,x.5 (also relating to the Wicked Priest): ''He will judge him with fire and brimstone.''

Hassidim, literally ''the Pious Ones''; the original behind the expression Hassidaeans and probably the basis of the Greek transliteration ''Essenes''; cf. *Anshei-Hesed* and the *Ebionei-Hesed* above.

Hesed, Piety; the first part of the *Hesed* and *Zedek* dichotomy, descriptive of man's rela-
    tionship to the Deity, *i.e.*, "thou shalt love the Lord thy God". Taken with the se-
    cond, "loving one's neighbor" or Righteousness towards one's fellow man, the two
    comprise the sum total of "the commands of *all Righteousness*" and epitomize the op-
    position ideological orientation; the root of the terminology *Hassidim*.
hittif, pouring out/spouting; as in CD,viii.13's "of Lying". For CD,i.14f. the Man of
    Jesting (or "the Comedian") "poured out on Israel the waters of Lying leading
    them astray in a void without a Way", which combines "Lying", "jesting",
    "spouting", and "leading astray" imageries with inverted allusion to "wilderness"
    and "Way" terminologies; see *Mattif/Mattif ha-Cazav*.
hok, statute or Law; at the heart of 1QS,viii-ix's exposition of Is 40:3's "Way in the
    wilderness", "the Way" being "the study of the Law". The phrase, "zealous for
    the Law", specifically occurs in ix.23 accompanied by reference to "the Day of
    Vengeance"; cf. *kin'at Mishpetei-Zedek* in iv.4. *N.b.*, CD,i.20's *yapheiru hok* to describe
    the "pursuit after" the *zaddik*—the synonym of 1QpHab,ii.6's *Mephirei ha-Brit*
    echoed too in 1QpHab,viii.17.
hon, Riches/wealth; one of CD,iv.17ff.'s "three nets of Belial"; in CD,vi.14ff. and viii.4ff.
    (including "fornication" imagery) directed against the establishment (probably
    Herodian); in 1QpHab,viii.10ff. and ix.4ff. related to the "gathering"/"robbing
    the Poor"/"profiteering from the Gentiles" activities of the Last Priests/Wicked
    Priest.
lechalah/lechalot, the language of destruction, applied in 1QpHab,xii.5f. to the conspiracy
    to destroy the Righteous Teacher and the Poor, *i.e.*, "as he plotted to destroy the
    Poor", so too would "God condemn him to destruction"; in this context
    synonymous with *leval'o/leval'am*.
leval'o/leval'am/teval'enu, the language of "swallowing"/"destruction"; applied in
    1QpHab,xi.5ff. to the confrontation between the Righteous Teacher and the Wicked
    Priest and the *destruction* of both. Its resonances with the Bela^c/Belial equivalence are
    purposeful, not to mention the "*hayil balla^c*" of 11QT,xlvi.10/Job 20:15 (*i.e.*,
    "swallowing wealth"). Cf. also "Balaam" as "swallower of the people" in b. San
    105a. In this sense, all aspects of the *B-L-^{c}* usage were considered illustrative of the
    activity most characterizing the Herodian establishment, *i.e.*, "swallowing".
losif, the language of gathering, applied in 1QpHab,viii.12 to the Wicked Priest's/last
    high priests' "gathering Riches" and "profiteering from the spoils of the Peoples"
    and a consonant harvest of blame.
ma'as, reject/deny/speak derogatorily about; a catchword for the legal posture of the Lying
    Spouter and those of his persuasion; in 1QpHab,v.11f. the former
    "rejected"/"spoke derogatorily about the Law in the midst of their entire congrega-
    tion." Cf. the parallel, more general, use in i.10, 1QS,iii.5f., and CD,vii.9,
    viii.18f., and 31f.
ma'asim/ma'aseihem, works/their works; generally works of the Law, paralleling the usage
    in the Letter of James and the use of *'amal* in 1QpHab and Is 53:11. Also used with
    inverted sense as in 1QpHab,x.11f.'s the Liar's "instructing them in Lying works"
    (*ma'asei-Sheker*) and 1QS,iv.23's *ma'asei-remiyyah*; also see *ma'asei-To'evot* in
    1QpHab,xii.8.
Ma'oz, Protection or Shield; in 1QH,vii.8ff. and 23ff. related to Fortress, strengthening,
    building, Wall, Foundations, Stone, and Cornerstone imagery; probably the basis of
    the *Oblias*/"Protection"/"Bulwark" allusion applied to James in early Church
    testimony and related to "Stone" and "Pillar" imagery in the N.T. generally.
Mattif/Mattif ha-Cazav, the Spouter/Pourer Out of Lying; a variation of the *Ish ha-Cazav*
    (the Man of Lying) and the *Ish ha-Lazon* (the Man of Jesting/Scoffing/Comedian) im-
    agery at Qumran, incorporating plays on what appear to have been his characteristic
    activities, pouring out words or waters (even perhaps speaking with his "Tongue"
    or "in tongues") and Lying.
Mephirei ha-Brit, Covenant-Breakers; synonymous with the *Bogdim*/House of Absalom in
    1QpHab,ii.1ff. and v.8ff., and related to the "breaking" charge in Ez 44:7ff. and Ja
    2:10ff. The opposite of 1QS,v.2ff.'s "sons of Zadok" as "Covenant-Keepers".

Migdal, Tower/Fortress/Bulwark; in 1QH,vii.8ff. applied together with the language of "Strength", "Stone", "Wall", "Cornerstone", building and Foundations imagery to the person of the Righteous Teacher.

Mishpat, Judgement; used in 1QpHab,v.4ff. in conjunction with *Beit ha-Mishpat* above; expressive of that Judgement God would make "through the hands of His Elect" (i.e., "the Bnei-Zadok" in CD,iv.3f.) on all Gentiles and backsliding Jews; cf. *Beit ha-Mishpat* above, *Yom ha-Mishpat* below, and 1QS,iv.4's *kinʾat Mishpetei-Zedek* ("zeal for the Judgements of Righteousness"—the opposite of 1QpHab,ix.1's *Mishpetei-Rishʿah*).

Moreh-Zedek/Moreh ha-Zedek, the Righteous Teacher or more literally, the Teacher of Righteousness.

nephesh-Zaddik (see also *nephesh-Ebion* and *nephesh-ʿAni,*), the soul of the *Zaddik*; terminology remounting to Is 53:11f. paralleling heart and body imagery generally at Qumran and in Ez 44:7ff., etc. Cf. CD,i.20 where *nephesh-Zaddik* is used synonymously with *Moreh ha-Zedek* and *nephesh-Ebion* and *nephesh-ʿAni* in 1QH,ii.32, iii.25, v.6, etc.

niddah/niddat, unclean/uncleanness; often used at Qumran in conjunction with the imagery of "*tumʾah*" (pollution), as for instance in 1QpHab,viii.13, CD,xii.1f., 1QS,iv.10 ("*darchei-niddah*", replete with "lying" and "fornication" imagery), and the Temple Scroll generally.

nilvu/nilvim, joined/Joiners; evoked in 4QpNah,iii.5 in relation to the *Petaʾei*-Ephraim and in eschatological exegesis of Ez 44:15 in CD,iv.3 (also echoed in 4QpNah,ii.9's *ger-nilveh*). Es 9:27 concretizes it as connotative of *Gentiles* "attaching themselves" to the Jewish Community, which in turn helps elucidate the Ephraim/City of Ephraim/Simple Ones of Ephraim usages. Probably synonymous in other vocabularies with the terminology "God-Fearers".

Nozrei ha-Brit/Nozrei Brito, the Keepers of His Covenant; cf. Ps 25:8ff., and Ps 119, where the expression is used synonymously with *Shomrei ha-Brit*—the qualitatively precise definition of "the sons of Zadok" in 1QS,v.2ff.; also *britcha yinzor* in Deut 33:9 and 4QTest. The allusions *Nozrim* (Hebrew terminology denoting "Christians") and "Zadokites" can be viewed, therefore, as variations on a theme.

ʿoseh ha-Torah/ʿOsei ha-Torah, doing *Torah*/the Doers of the *Torah*; the expression *ʿOsei ha-Torah* limits the soteriological scope of the exegeses of Hab 2:3 and 2:4 in 1QpHab,vii.11ff. to *Torah-Doers in the House of Judah*. "Doers"/"doing"/ "Breakers"/"keeping" usages are also reflected in the language of Ja 1:22ff. *ʿOseh ha-Torah* defines xii.4f.'s "*Petaʾei*-Yehudah," distinguishing it from 4QpNah,iii's "*Petaʾei*-Ephraim" and tying it to the "Keepers of the Covenant" terminology. The root of *maʿaseh/maʿasim*.

Petaʾei-Yehudah/*Petaʾei*-Ephraim, the Simple Ones of Judah/Simple Ones of Ephraim; in 1QpHab,xii.4f. the former are the "*Torah*-doing" community rank and file. In 4QpNa,iii.5f. the latter must be associated with Gentile *nilvim*, who, it is hoped, "will once again join themselves to Israel" (cf. *ger-nilveh* in ii.9). In 8f. they are associated with being led astray by "Deceivers...teaching their Lies, a Tongue of their Lies, deceitful lips, and misleading the Many". Cf. also the use of "Little Ones" and "Samaritans" in the N.T.

Rabbim, the Many, used at Qumran to designate the rank and file of the community, who were presumably the beneficiaries of the justifying activities (whether via suffering works or imparted Knowledge) of the Righteous Teacher/Community Council; the usage goes back to the vocabulary of Is 53:11f.—cf. also its use in the Dn 12 passage noted above. Its sense is reversed in 1QpHab,x.11's "wearing out Many with worthless work" and 4QpNah,ii.8's "leading Many astray" both relating to activities of the Liar.

Rashaʿ/Reshaʿim, Evil/Evil Ones; usually connected in the *pesharim* to the Wicked Priest, but sometimes, as in 1QpHab,v.9f., to the Man of Lying.

remiyyah, deceit; in 1QS,viii.22 and ix.8 tied to covert infractions of the Law and in 1QS,viii.22ff., ix.8ff. (reflected in CD,viii.30) to consonant bans on work, table fellowship, or common purse; cf. "deceit"/"deceitful works" in 1QS,iv.9 and 23 and "deceitful lips" in 4QpNah,ii.8.

Rishonim, the First; to be viewed in conjunction with allusions to "the Last" and resonating with N.T. parodies of both; in CD,i,4ff. and iv.9, specifically denoting the *Zaddikim* of old (or "the Forefathers") with whom God made the first Covenant.

Ruah-Emet, in 1QS,iv.21 (amid allusion to baptism, etc.), Spirit of Truth; a variation of the language of the Holy Spirit. In viii.12 this relationship to "the Holy Spirit" is made explicit. Also to be viewed in the context of several contraries more or less typifying "the Spirit" of the Lying Scoffer, *i.e.*, Lying, fornication, insults, Evil, Darkness, etc.; cf. 1QS,iv.9ff.

shavo, worthless; in 1QpHab,x.10f. used to characterize the community's perception of the Liar's activities, *i.e.*, "the worthless city" and the "worthless service with which he tires out Many" (cf. Ja 1:26 on his "worthless religion", "heart of deceit", and "Tongue").

Sheker/ma⁽asei-Sheker, Lying/works of Lying; the terminology is part and parcel of the lying/spouting/boasting imagery at Qumran. Often accompanied by allusion to "the Tongue" or "lips" and used in conjunction with reference to "works," baptismal imagery, or "leading astray".

Shomrei ha-Brit, Keepers of the Covenant, 1QS,iv.2ff.'s qualitatively precise definition of "the Sons of Zadok", harking back to allusions in Ez 44:6ff, and Psalms; *n.b.*, the parallel represented by *Nozrei-Brito* and the contrast represented by *Mephirei ha-Brit*.

Tamim/Tamimim, the Perfect; also sometimes, Perfection—a fundamental notion at Qumran based on references to Noah in Gn 6:9 as "Righteous and Perfect in his generation"; the relationship to parallel N.T. notation (cf. Mt 5:48, 19:21, Ja 1:4, 17, 25, 2:22, etc.) is intrinsic.

To⁽evot, Abominations—*darchei-To⁽evot* in 1QpHab,viii.12f. Here and in xii.8, those of the Wicked Priest, particularly his pollution of the Temple/Temple Treasure through violent tax-collecting and "robbing the Poor". Part and parcel of the language of "polluting the Temple"/"breaking the Covenant" in Ez 44:6ff.; in the Temple Scroll, related to forbidden foods (xlviii.6), marriage with nieces (lxvi.11ff.; also referred to as "*niddah*"), and Gentiles (lx.17ff. and lxii.16).

Tom, Perfect/Perfection; *Tom-Derech/Tamimei-Derech*. Perfection of the Way/the Perfect of the Way; also linked to expressions based on Is 40:3 like *Yisharei-Derech*, "the Straight" or "Upright of the Way".

tum'ah/teme' ha-Mikdash/yitame' et Mikdash-El, pollution/pollution of the Sanctuary of God, generally tied to a demand for "separation" (cf. 11QT,xlvi.9ff. and CD,iv.17ff.); with *To⁽evot* part and parcel of the charges relating to the admission of foreigners into the Temple in Ez 44:7, as well as in consonant "Zadokite"/"Zealot" ideologies. As used in 1QpHab,xii.8f., directed against the Wicked Priest who did not "circumcize the foreskin of his heart" (Ez 44:9), and in viii.13, 1QS,v.19f., and CD,xii.1f. linked to *niddah*.

yazdik-zaddik (yazdiku-zaddikim), the "justification" ideology at Qumran based on the terminology of Is 53:11 (and to a lesser extent, Is 5:23); cf. also its use in Dn 12:3 above and see *Zaddik* and *zedakah* below.

yazzilem/yazzilum, save them/be saved; the language of salvation, associated with the language of the "House of Judgement"/"Day of Judgement". The first in 1QpHab,viii.1f.'s exegesis of Hab 2:4 refers to the "salvation of the Righteous"; the second in xii.14ff., the condemnation of "the servants of idols (Gentile idolators) and Evil Ones" (here backsliding Jews; cf. 2 Pe 2:9 and 3:7).

yehalluhu, pollute it. This plural usage is attached to the singular allusion to Bela⁽ in 11QT,xlvi.11 and forms the background to "the Zadokite Statement" in Ez 44:6ff., where the ban on "bringing strangers uncircumcised in heart and flesh into My Temple to pollute it" is enunciated.

yeter ha-⁽amim, the other or additional ones of the Gentiles; in 1QpHab,ix.7 specifically identified with "the Army of the *Kittim*", *i.e.*, the Romans; see *⁽amim*.

yikboz, gathering; in 1QpHab,viii.11 and ix.5 having to do with the *darchei-To'evot* or "gathering" activities of the Wicked Priest/Last Priests via the instrument of Unruly Gentiles; in this context "gathering" wealth—see also *losif*.

Yom ha-Mishpat, Day of Judgement, linking up with the usages *Mishpat/Beit ha-Mishpat* and *yazzilem/yazzilum* and used eschatologically in 1QpHab,xii.14 and xiii.2f., *i.e.*, "on the Day of Judgement God would destroy all the Idolators and Evil Ones from the Earth".

Zaddik/Zaddikim, the Righteous/the Righteous One(s); the terminology is highly developed in Jewish *Kabbalah* and Jewish resurrection theory. Via the Is 53:11 *yazdik-zaddik* conceptuality, the basis of "justification" theorizing, Qumran's esoteric exegesis of Ez 44:15, and the "purist Sadducee" movement.

zamam/zammu, conspired; in 1QpHab,xii.6 relating to the Wicked Priest's *judicial* conspiracy to destroy the Righteous Teacher/Poor/Simple of Judah doing *Torah*. In 1QH,iv.7ff. the usage applies to both "the sons of Belial" (Herodians) and their "nets", not to mention all "Scoffers of Deceit"/"Scoffers of Lying" (*Malizei-Chazav*) who lead the people astray "with Smooth Things", "give vinegar to the thirsty", and whose "works are boasting".

zanut, fornication, one of "the three nets of Belial"; in CD,iv.17ff. marrying nieces and divorce; in viii.5 tied to "Riches" and incest. Part and parcel of James' directives to overseas communities (cf. too Ja 1:14f., 4:1ff., and Re 2:14), the imagery of which pervades Qumran; *e.g.*, 1QS,iv.10's "zeal for lustfulness, *ma'asei-To'evot* in a spirit of *zanut*, and *darchei-niddah* in the service of pollution" and *par contra* 1QpHab,v.4ff.'s Elect of God "not lusting after their eyes" (cf. 2 Pe 2:13f.).

Zedek, Righteousness; with *Hesed*, the fundamental notation at Qumran. Taken together these two represent the basic ideological orientation of all opposition groups in the Second Temple period; the second of the two "all Righteousness" commandments, *i.e.*, "loving one's neighbor as oneself" or Righteousness towards one's fellow man, which moves easily into a consonant demand for economic equality and an insistence on poverty.

zedakah, also translated as Righteousness, but having the form of a verbal noun implying something of the sense of "justification", *i.e.*, in place of sacrifice, one "was justified" by charity.

GENERAL INDEX

Aaron, Messiah of, 91
Abba Hilkiah, 54
Abba Joseph b. Hanin, 44
Abot de R. Nathan, 6, 17, 34, 66
abeit-galuto, 50, 62f., 67
Abominations, 9, 18, 35, 46f., 49, 67, 69f.,
  88f., 91; *see To*ᶜ*evot*
Abraham, 41, 54
Acts, viii, 4f., 9f., 17, 19, 22, 30, 33, 58f.,
  62, 76, 92f.; James and Jerusalem
  Council in, 28, 31, 33, 36, 56, 65, 76,
  93; Qumran terminology, 24f., 32, 37,
  88; on Simon in Caesarea, viii, 5, 10, 33
Adiabene, 30, *see* Helen
adoptionist sonship, 5, 55
Adversary, *see* Enemy
Agrippa I, 12, 21, 27, 59, 66, 81, 88ff.;
  confrontation with Simon, 9f., 33, 51,
  61, 90; kinsman of Saulus, 10, 47
Agrippa II, 9, 14, 27, 35, 44, 59, 64, 97ff.;
  barred from Jerusalem by "the Inno-
  vators", 9, 22, 51, 53, 89, 91; and
  James' death, 8, 10, 14, 56, 62, 65;
  kinsman of Saulus, 4; and Temple
  wall, 9f., 14, 19, 51, 87, 90
Aharoni, Y., 84
Aharonim, 37
Albright, W. F., 12, 85
Alexander Jannaeus, 14f.
Allegro, J. M., 66
ᶜ*am/*ᶜ*amim*, vii, 76ff., 87, 89, 91, 93
ᶜ*amal/*ᶜ*amalam*, 22, 32, 35, 40ff., 53f., 57,
  60; *see* works
amanatam, 42, *see* faith
ᶜ*amod/*ᶜ*omdim*, 66, 71; *see* stand
Anabathmoi Jacobou, 18f.
Anan ben David, 8
Ananias, 18, 42ff.
Ananus b. Ananus, viii, 8f., 16ff., 19, 26,
  28, 35, 43f., 49ff., 60, 67, 71, 89; independent ruler, 13f.; and James, 10,
  28, 42f., 50f., 62, 65; corruption/
  profiteering of, 28, 43f., 48
ᶜ*Ani/*ᶜ*Aniyyim/*ᶜ*Anavim*, 11, 42, 44, 66ff.,
  71; ᶜ*Anavei-Arez*, 66, 68; *see* Meek
animal(s), 92f.; *see be*ᶜ*ir*
Anshei-(H)amas, 65; *see* Violent Ones
Anshei-Hesed, 7, 37
Anshei Kodesh-Tamim, 7, 37
Anshei-Remiyyah, 57, *see* deceit
Antigonus, 51

Antioch, 30, 33
archaeology, vii, x, 13ff., 28, 49, 75-85;
  coins, 12, 21, 76ff., 81ff.
Archapostles, 21
Aristobulus II, 15
Aristobulus b. Herod of Chalcis, 10, 59, 66
ᶜ*Arizim/*ᶜ*Arizei-Go*ʾ*im*, 22, 26f., 30ff., 46f.,
  64, 71, 93; *see* Violent Ones
Armenia, 10, 59
Asia, 93
Assumption of Moses, 80
atonement, 19, 56, 65; at Qumran, 8, 19,
  23, 33, 37, 65; by James, 3, 5, 8, 26,
  49, 61f.
Avigad, N., 2, 85
ᶜ*Avlah*, 53, 73
ᶜ*avodah*, 54, 57; ᶜ*avodat-shavo*, 54, 73; *see*
  works
ᶜ*Azat-Emet/*ᶜ*azatam*, see ᶜ*ezah*

backsliders, 18f., 28f., 42, 49, 53, 72f., 79
Balaam, 62, 90-94
Balak, 93
*balla*ᶜ, ixf., 18, 37f., 67, 90, 92
Banus, 4, 15, 36, 45
baptism, 5, 23, 76; imagery of, 23, 30,
  52ff., 60f.
Bar Kochba, 77, 82ff.
barring the door, 88
Barnabas, 30f.
bathing, 4, 15, 45
beheading, 51
*be*ᶜ*ir*, 92; *see* Beᶜor
Beit ha-Mishpat, 40ff., 52, 65, 72; *see*
  Mishpat, Yom ha-Mishpat
*Beit-Ya*ᶜ*acov*, 11, 66
Beit-Yehudah, 37, 39
*Bela*ᶜ, ixf., 18, 20, 67, 87, 90-94
Belial, x, 14f., 22, 62, 90-94; three nets
  of, viii, 9, 67, 80, 87ff., 90; *see* fornica-
  tion, Riches
Beliar, *see* Belial
belief/believing, ix, 24, 26, 31, 38, 41f., 71
Bene Hezir, tomb of, 18, 85; *see* Boethu-
  sians
Benjamin/Benjaminites, 90ff., *see* also
  Belial
Beᶜor/*be*ᶜ*orot*, 90-94; *see* also "things sacri-
  ficed to idols"
Bethlehem, 82
*beza*ᶜ, 43; *see* robbing